PINK FLOYD

60 YEARS

Alison James

sona
BOOKS

sona BOOKS

First published in the UK 2022 by Sona Books an imprint of Danann Media Publishing Ltd
This updated extended version published in the UK 2026 by Danann Media Publishing Ltd

CAT NO: SON0720
Photography courtesy of

Getty images:

- Andrew Whittuck/Redferns
- Adam Ritchie/Redferns
- GAB Archive/Redferns
- Michael Ochs Archives
- Ullstein Bild
- Silver Screen Collection
- Bernard Allemane / INA
- Gijsbert Hanekroot/Redferns
- Nik Wheeler/Sygma
- Pete Still/Redferns
- Ross Marino
- Rahman Hassani/SOPA Images/LightRocket
- Tim Hall/Redferns
- Chip HIRES/Gamma-Rapho
- Jo Hale
- John D McHugh/AFP
- Mick Gold

Alamy images:

- dcphoto
- f8 archive
- Blueee
- Pictorial Press Ltd
- MediaPunch Inc
- INTERFOTO
- The Vintage Papers
- Odile Noël
- Retro AdArchives
- Everett Collection, Inc.
- Lebrecht Music & Arts
- Neil Baylis
- Posters
- Associated Press
- PA Images

Book layout & design Darren Grice at Ctrl-d and Alex Young at Cre81ve
Copy Editor Tom O'Neill

Made in EU.
ISBN: 978-1-917259-78-1

CONTENTS

INTRODUCTION

'We did all sorts of strange things for live concerts'

David Gilmour

From their avant-garde, art-schoolesque psychedelic sound and light shows of the 1960s through to their technicolour, 'flying-pig', off-the-scale stadium spectaculars of the '70s, '80s and '90s, Pink Floyd's lavish stage shows – combining intense visual experiences with extraordinary music amplified through ground-breaking quadrophonic surround sound – were works of true creative genius. Never satisfied with producing *'the same old show'* year after year, the Floyd's mantra was always *'bigger, better, more'* where live performances were concerned – the aim being to give their audiences a larger-than-life experience for all the senses that they would never forget. If there's one thing Syd Barrett (in the early days at any rate), Roger Waters, David Gilmour, Nick Mason and Richard Wright knew how to do, it was put on a show...

Back L-R: Syd Barrett, Nick Mason. Front L-R: Roger Waters, Rick Wright, 1967

THE SYD BARRETT YEARS

'I'm full of dust and guitars'

Syd Barrett

Cambridge, England... Ancient university town and esteemed seat of learning set in England's flat-as-a-pancake fenlands – and the birthplace of what would become the genesis of 'Pink Floyd', one of the most experimental yet successful bands in rock history.

Roger Barrett (born January 6 1946) and Roger Waters (born September 6 1943) first laid eyes on each other in the early 1950s as small boys attending Morley Memorial School in the south east of the city. Being` three years apart, they had little to do with each other although both signed up for Saturday morning art classes at a local teacher training college where Barrett happened to befriend a certain David Gilmour (born March 6 1946).

Aged 11, Barrett followed Waters to the Cambridgeshire High School for Boys. Gilmour attended a different secondary school, although he and Barrett would meet up outside school and share their love of art – and music. By the age of 15, Roger Barrett had become 'Syd', gleaning the nickname from a bass player in a local jazz band who was called Sid Barrett. Aged 16, both boys started at Cambridge Technical College.

'We would hang around in the art department, playing guitars every lunchtime,' Gilmour was to recall. *'We were teaching each other basically. The thing with Syd was that his guitar wasn't his strongest feature. His style was very stiff. I always thought I was the better guitar player. But he was very clever, very intelligent – an artist in every way. And he was a frightening talent when it came to words and lyrics. They just used to pour out.'*

By now, Barrett and Gilmour were socialising with Roger Waters, and it was after a trip to see Gene Vincent in London in 1961 that Waters and Barrett discussed the band that they one day hoped to form. In autumn 1962, Waters moved to London in order to study architecture at the Regent Street Polytechnic and it was here he met fellow students, Nick Mason (born January 27 1944) and Rick Wright (born July 28 1943) who would go on to play drums and keyboards, respectively, in 'Pink Floyd'. Meanwhile Barrett and Gilmour remained in Cambridge. Gilmour joined a band called 'The Newcomers' and Barrett played with local outfits, 'Those Without' and 'Geoff Mott & The Mottoes.'

At the age of 18, in late summer 1964, Barrett made the move to London to go to Camberwell Art College.

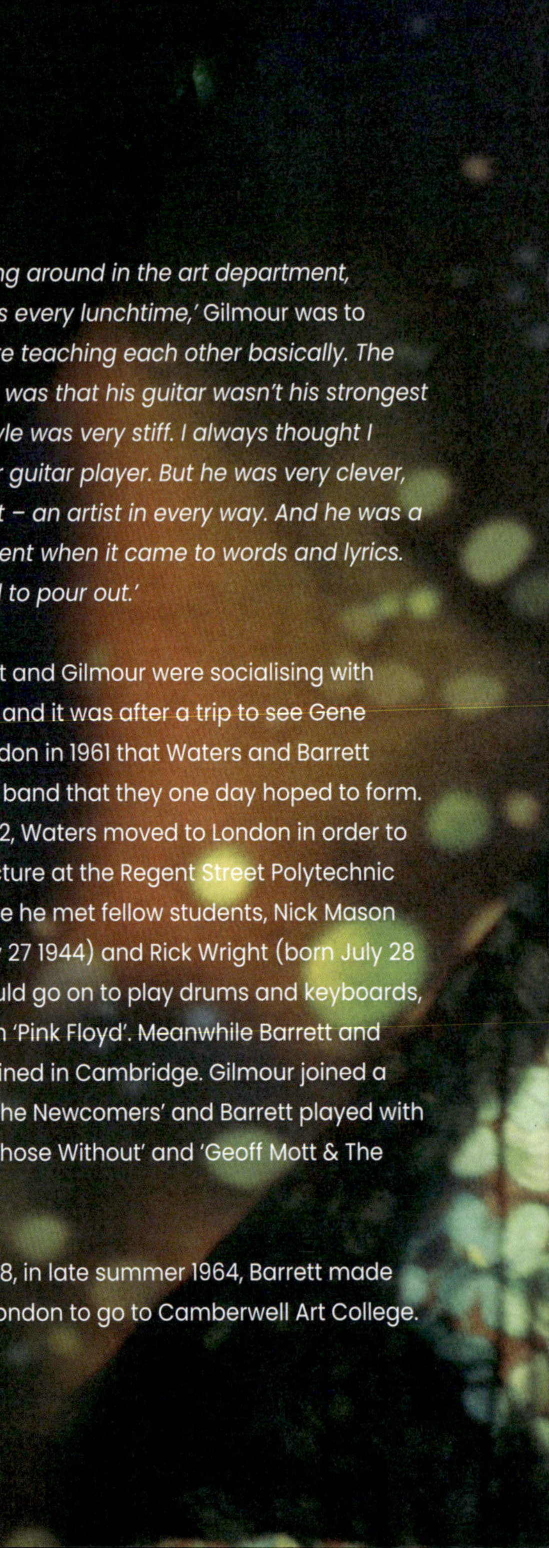

Singer Syd Barrett performing live onstage, 1967

He was offered a place in a shared house with Roger Waters and two other Cambridge friends, Dave Gilbert and Bob Klose.

'I was living in Highgate with Roger, we shared a place there, and got a van and spent a lot of our grant on pubs and that sort on thing,' Barrett would go on to say. *'We were interested in playing guitars and played Stones' numbers.'*

Roger had formed a rhythm and blues band with Nick Mason, Rick Wright, and blues-guitar supremo Klose. Known at various times and incarnations as 'Sigma 6', 'The Meggadeaths', 'The Abdabs', 'The Screaming Abdabs' and 'The Tea Set', Syd joined the band as rhythm guitarist during the 'Tea Set' phase. Shortly afterwards, the Pink Floyd name first came into being, derived by Syd when the band heard there was another combo called 'The Tea Set'. His inspiration came from two obscure blues musicians, Pink Anderson and Floyd Council, whose records he had in his collection. A fourth Cantabrigian, vocalist Chris Dennis, completed the line-up.

It's believed that the first gig ever played by the band as 'Pink Floyd', or rather 'The Pink Floyd Sound' as they were initially known, was at 'The Countdown' coffee and wine bar, in Kensington, west London in February

A psychedelic light show as Pink Floyd perform at the UFO Club, London, December 1966

1965. They performed three 90-minute sets of rhythm and blues numbers and were paid just £15. By that summer, six had become four with Dennis quitting to join the RAF and Bob Klose leaving to concentrate fully on his university studies. Waters, Barrett, Mason and Wright remained as students although art and architecture were ceasing to be priorities *'It was a major switch when Bob left the band,'* recalls Nick Mason. *'That sent us spiralling into another direction. Syd and Roger were listening to John Mayall and Alexis Korner but somewhere along the line, Syd had discovered writing songs and his songs were not in that vein at all.'*

Waters agrees and says The Who's Pete Townsend was a major influence on Barrett.

'Those noises that Pete Townsend was making then. . .the squeaks and feedback. That influenced Syd. So, we started making strange noises instead of playing blues.'

'Pink Floyd' played a handful of gigs over the rest of the year but it wasn't really until 1966 that the band began gigging regularly, showcasing their experimental sound and innovative light effects which were influenced by Syd Barrett's experimentation with lysergic acid diethylamide – better known as hallucinogenic drug LSD or Acid.

1966

'The Pink Floyd were the only psychedelic band. They had this improvisation, this spirit of psychedelia which I don't think any other band had. They didn't play chords. At their finest it was very, extraordinary free improvisation'

Peter Jenner, future manager

9 Jan	The Goings On, Archer Street, London, England
11 Mar	Rag Ball, Concourse Area, University of Essex, Wivenhoe Park, Colchester, England
12 Mar	Rag Ball, Concourse Area, University of Essex, Wivenhoe Park, Colchester, England
13 Mar	Spontaneous Underground, The Marquee, Wardour Street, London, England
27 Mar	Spontaneous Underground, The Marquee, Wardour Street, London, England
3 Apr	Spontaneous Underground, The Marquee, Wardour Street, London, England
17 Apr	Spontaneous Underground, The Marquee, Wardour Street, London, England
1 May	Spontaneous Underground, The Marquee, Wardour Street, London, England

8 May Spontaneous Underground, The Marquee, Wardour Street, London, England

15 May Spontaneous Underground, The Marquee, Wardour Street, London, England

5 Jun Spontaneous Underground, The Marquee, Wardour Street, London, England

12 Jun Spontaneous Underground, The Marquee, Wardour Street, London, England

30 Sep London Free School, All Saints Church Hall, Powis Gardens, London, England

14 Oct London Free School, All Saints Church Hall, Powis Gardens, London, England

15 Oct International Times First All Night Rave, The Roundhouse, Chalk Farm, London, England

19 Oct Top Rank Suite, Brighton, England

21 Oct London Free School, All Saints Church Hall, Powis Gardens, London, England

28 Oct London Free School, All Saints Church Hall, Powis Gardens, London, England

4 Nov London Free School, All Saints Church Hall, Powis Gardens, London, England

5 Nov Wilton Hall, Bletchley, England

5 Nov The Clubhouse, Fiveacres Country Club, Bricket Wood, near Watford, England (private party)

8 Nov London Free School, All Saints Church Hall, Powis Gardens, London, England

11 Nov London Free School, All Saints Church Hall, Powis Gardens, London, England

12 Nov Corn Exchange, Bedford, England

13 Nov Starlite Ballroom, Greenford, England

15 Nov London Free School, All Saints Church Hall, Powis Gardens, London, England

18 Nov Rooms A&B, Hornsey College of Art, Hornsey, London, England

19 Nov Main Hall, Technical College, Canterbury, England

22 Nov London Free School, All Saints Church Hall, Powis Gardens, London, England

29 Nov London Free School, All Saints Church Hall, Powis Gardens, London, England

3 Dec Psychodelphia versus Ian Smith, The Roundhouse, Chalk Farm, London, England

8 Dec Chicago Christmas Dance, Royal College Of Art, Kensington, London, England

12 Dec You're Joking – A Benefit Carnival for Oxfam, Royal Albert Hall, Kensington, London, England

16 Dec AA Students Christmas Carnival, The Architects Association, Bedford Square, London, England

20 Dec Art School Psychedelic Freak Out, Cambridgeshire College of Art and Technology, Cambridge, England

22 Dec The Marquee, Wardour Street, London, England

23 Dec UFO, The Blarney Club, Tottenham Court Road, London, England

29 Dec The Marquee, Wardour Street, London, England

30 Dec UFO, The Blarney Club, Tottenham Court Road, London, England

31 Dec New Year's Eve All Night Rave, The Roundhouse, Chalk Farm, London, England

PINK FLOYD
MARCH 15 66
MARQUEE
90 WARDOUR ST.
LONDON W.1.
7:30-11:00

'Who will be there? Poets, pop singers, hoods, Americans, homosexuals (because they make up 10% of the population), 20 clowns, jazz musicians, one murderer, jazz musicians, sculptors, politicians and some girls who defy description are among those invited'

PR material for The Spontaneous Underground at the Marquee Club, Soho, London, UK, Spring 1966.

From March 1966, 'The Pink Floyd Sound' were regulars at the Spontaneous Underground 'happening' on Sunday afternoons at the legendary Marquee Club. It was now that the whole 'mixed media' thing started happening for them with a never-seen-before combination of avant-garde music and art.

'Sunday afternoons at the Marquee with us banging and crashing away, with filming going in the background,' as Roger Waters put it.

The exotic light show was put together by two San Franciscans from the hippie Haight-Ashbury district of the US city and, with its innovative use of coloured slides, was light years away from standard theatrical lighting systems of the time. It was at the Marquee that *'London's loudest electronic beat group'*, as one reviewer dubbed them, were spotted by future manager, Peter Jenner, then a lecturer in economics.

'It was one of the first rock events I'd seen – I didn't know anything about rock, really,' he has admitted. *'Actually, the Floyd then were barely semi-pro standard, now that I think about it, but I was so impressed by the electric guitar sound. At that stage, they were a blues band who played things like "Louie Louie" and then played wacky bits in the middle. So, the solos were wacky, they just sort of went on – this was Syd Barrett and also Rick Wright. I wandered around the stage, trying to work out where the noise was coming from, just what was playing it. Normally, you would hear something and think, "That's the bass, that's the drums, that's the sax"... you knew where everything was. But The Floyd, when they were doing their solo bits, I couldn't work out whether it was coming from the keyboards or from the guitar, and that was what was interesting to me. I tracked 'em down and they said, "What we really need is a manager, otherwise we're going to break up. We don't have enough equipment and we need someone to help". I called my friend Andrew King, who already worked in the music industry, and we became their managers.'*

Under the guidance of Blackhill Enterprises, the company Jenner and King swiftly formed together, the band, now known as 'The Pink Floyd', began performing on London's underground music scene, notably at a venue booked by the London Free School in Notting Hill. By October 1966, the band were playing more of Barrett's songs, which would later feature on Pink Floyd's first album. Their relationship with Blackhill Enterprises was strengthened when they became full partners, each with an unprecedented one-sixth share. More gigs followed, including one at a Catholic youth club whose owner refused to pay. At a magistrates' court a judge agreed with the owner, who claimed that the band's performance *'wasn't music'*. This was not the only occasion on which they encountered such entrenched opinions, but they were better received at the UFO Club in London. They enjoyed playing there, and used the in-house lighting to good effect. As time went on, the lighting became even more experimental. Peter Wynne-Wilson, a lighting technician friend of Syd's, was now in-charge. One of his early gimmicks involved stretching a condom over a wire frame and dripping oil onto it, through which light would then be shone creating one of the first oil slide effects. This was to become a defining feature of the band's live gigs. Their gigs were 'sonic freak-outs' – half hidden by these experimental light shows and projections. Pink Floyd were one of the first bands to use a dedicated travelling light show in conjunction with their performances. Dynamic liquid light shows were projected onto enormous screens behind the band while they played. Strobe lights were also incorporated, controlled manually by an engineer. This had the effect of totally obscuring the band apart from their shadows. Barrett took advantage of this – holding up his arms and making his shadow grow, shrink and undulate. It was a truly visual spectacle. Simultaneously, his spacey lead guitar swept over Waters' trance-like bass as Wright and Mason created a surrounding soundscape.

By the close of 1966, the band were contemplating giving up their studies to concentrate on their budding careers as ground-breaking musicians. It had been an eventful year but '67 would prove to be totally 'mind-blowing'. For Syd Barrett most of all.

A psychedelic light show as Pink Floyd perform at the UFO Club, London, December 1966

1967

'We may have been the darlings of London but out in the suburbs it was fairly terrible. Before "See Emily Play", we'd have things thrown at us on stage. After "See Emily Play", it was screaming girls wanting to hear our hit song'

Peter Jenner

Typical set list:

DawnMatilda MotherFlamingThe ScarecrowSee Emily PlayBikeArnold LayneCandy and a Currant BunPow R. Toc H.Interstellar OverdriveBubblesLucifer SamTake Up Thy Stethoscope and WalkGnomeReaction in GAstronomy DomineScream Thy Last Scream

5 Jan	The Marquee, Wardour Street, London, England
6 Jan	Freak Out Ethel, Seymour Hall, Paddington, London, England
8 Jan	The Upper-Cut, Forest Gate, London, England
13 Jan	UFO, The Blarney Club, Tottenham Court Road, London, England (The Pink Floyd – London 66-67, video)
14 Jan	Coming-up Hop, The Great Hall, University of Reading, Reading, England
16 Jan	Institute of Contemporary Arts, Mayfair, London, England
17 Jan	Music In Colour By The Pink Floyd, Commonwealth Institute, Kensington, London, England
19 Jan	The Marquee, Wardour Street, London, England
20 Jan	UFO, The Blarney Club, Tottenham Court Road, London, England
21 Jan	The Birdcage Club, Eastney, Portsmouth, England
27 Jan	UFO, The Blarney Club, Tottenham Court Road, London, England (Scene Special, Granada TV, broadcast 7 Mar)
28 Jan	Hexagon Restaurant, University of Essex, Wivenhoe Park, Colchester, England
2 Feb	Cadenas, Stoke Hotel, Guildford, England
3 Feb	Queen's Hall, Leeds, England
9 Feb	New Addington Hotel, New Addington, Croydon, England
10 Feb	Leicester College of Art & Technology, Leicester, England
11 Feb	Falmer House, University of Sussex, Brighton, England
17 Feb	St Catherine's College Valentine Ball, The Dorothy Ballroom, Cambridge, England
18 Feb	California Ballroom, Dunstable, England
20 Feb	Adelphi Ballroom, West Bromwich, England
24 Feb	Ricky Tick Club, Thames Hotel, Windsor, England (rescheduled to 25 Mar)
24 Feb	UFO Club, Tottenham Court Road, London, England (Die Jungen Nachtwandler – London Unter 21, Beyerischer Rundfunk TV, broadcast 3 Jul)
25 Feb	Ricky Tick Club, Hounslow, England (rescheduled to 24 Mar)
28 Feb	Blaises Club, Imperial Hotel, Kensington, London, England
1 Mar	The Ballroom, Eel Pie Island Hotel, Twickenham, England
2 Mar	Assembly Rooms, Worthing, England
3 Mar	Market Hall, St. Albans, England
3 Mar	UFO, The Blarney Club, Tottenham Court Road, London, England
4 Mar	Poly Rag Ball, Regent Street Polytechnic, London, England
5 Mar	Saville Theatre, Shaftesbury Avenue, London, England
6 Mar	Granada TV Studios, Manchester, England (The Rave, pilot TV programme, not broadcast)
7 Mar	Winter Gardens, Malvern, England
9 Mar	The Marquee, Wardour Street, London, England
10 Mar	UFO, The Blarney Club, Tottenham Court Road, London, England
11 Mar	Main Hall, Technical College, Canterbury, England
12 Mar	Agincourt Ballroom, Camberley, England
17 Mar	Kingston Technical College, Kingston-Upon-Thames, England
18 Mar	Enfield College of Technology, Enfield, London, England
22 Mar	Canteen, London School of Economics, London, England
23 Mar	Clifton Hall, Rotherham, England
24 Mar	Ricky Tick Club, Hounslow, England
25 Mar	Ricky Tick Club, Thames Hotel, Windsor, England
25 Mar	New Yorker Discotheque, Swindon, England
26 Mar	Shoreline Club, Caribbean Hotel, Bognor Regis, England (early hours 26 Mar)
28 Mar	Chinese R&B Jazz Club, Bristol Corn Exchange, Bristol, England
29 Mar	The Ballroom, Eel Pie Island Hotel, Twickenham, England (cancelled)
31 Mar	Top Spot Ballroom, Ross-on-Wye, England
1 Apr	The Birdcage Club, Eastney, Portsmouth, England
3 Apr	Playhouse Theatre, Northumberland Avenue, London, England (Monday! Monday! BBC Light, live broadcast)
6 Apr	City Hall, Salisbury, England
7 Apr	Floral Hall, Belfast, Northern Ireland
8 Apr	Rhodes Center, Bishops Stortford, England

8 Apr The Roundhouse, Chalk Farm, London, England

9 Apr Britannia Rowing Club, Nottingham, England

10 Apr The Pavilion, Bath, England

13 Apr Railway Club, Tilbury, England

15 Apr K4 Discotheque, West Pier, Brighton, England

16 Apr The Brady Club, Stepney, London, England

19 Apr Bromel Club, Court Hotel, Bromley, England

20 Apr Queen's Hall, Barnstable, England

21 Apr Starlight Ballroom, Greenford, England

21 Apr UFO, The Blarney Club, Tottenham Court Road, London, England

22 Apr Sixty Nine Club, Royal York Hotel, Ryde, Isle of Wight, England (cancelled)

22 Apr Benn Memorial Hall, Rugby, England

23 Apr Starlight Ballroom, Crawley, England

24 Apr Blue Opera Club, The Feathers Public House, Ealing Broadway, London, England

25 Apr The Stage Club, Clarendon Restaurant, Oxford, England

28 Apr Tabernacle Club, Hillgate, Stockport, England

29 Apr VARA TV Studios, Zaandam, The Netherlands (Fan Club, Nederland 1 TV, broadcast 5 May)

29 Apr 14 Hour Technicolour Dream, Alexandra Palace, London, England

29 Apr St. George's Ballroom, Hinckley, England (cancelled and rescheduled to 13 May)

30 Apr Plaza Teen Club, Thornton Lodge Hall, Huddersfield, England

3 May The Moulin Rouge, Ainsdale, England

4 May Locarno Ballroom, Coventry, England

6 May Kitson College, Leeds, England

7 May Mojo Club, Tollbar, Sheffield, England

12 May Games For May, Queen Elizabeth Hall, London, England

13 May St. George's Ballroom, Hinckley, England

14 May BBC Lime Grove Studios, Shepherds Bush, London, England (Look of the Week, BBC2 TV, live broadcast)

19 May Club A Go-Go, Newcastle-upon-Tyne, England

20 May Floral Hall, Southport, England

21 May Regent Ballroom, Brighton, England (cancelled)

23 May Town Hall, High Wycombe, England

24 May Bromel Club, Court Hotel, Bromley, England

25 May Gwent Constabulary ('A' Division) Spring Holiday Barn Dance, The Barn, Grosmont Wood Farm,

Cross Ash, Wales

26 May General Post Office North West Regional Dance, Empress Ballroom, Winter Gardens, Blackpool, England

27 May Civic Hall, Nantwich, England

29 May Barbecue '67, Tulip Bulb Auction Hall, Spalding, England

2 Jun UFO, The Blarney Club, Tottenham Court Road, London, England

9 Jun College of Art, Hull, England

9 Jun UFO, The Blarney Club, Tottenham Court Road, London, England

10 Jun The Nautilus Club, South Pier, Lowestoft, England

11 Jun Patronaatsgebouw, Terneuzen, The Netherlands (cancelled)

11 Jun Concertgebouw, Vlissingen, The Netherlands (cancelled)

13 Jun Blue Opera Club, The Feathers Public House, Ealing Broadway, London, England

16 Jun Tiles Club, Oxford Street, London, England

17 Jun The Ballroom, Dreamland Amusement Park, Margate, England (early show)

17 Jun Supreme Ballroom, Ramsgate, England (late show)

18 Jun Radio London Motor Racing & Pop Festival, Brands Hatch Race Track, Brands Hatch, England

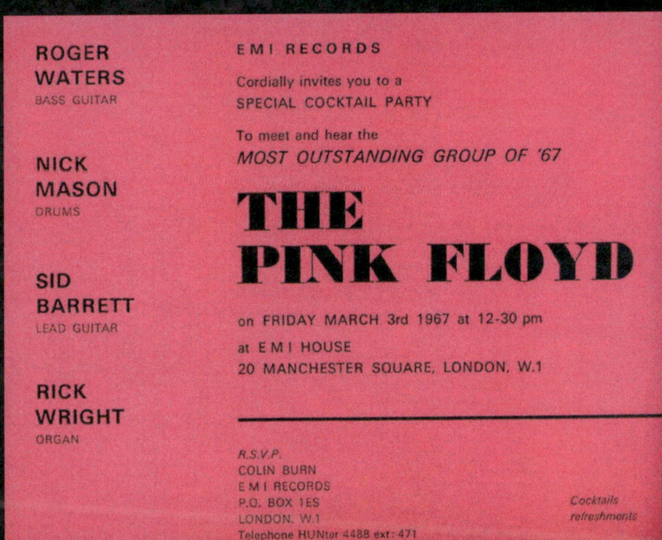
ROGER WATERS
BASS GUITAR

NICK MASON
DRUMS

SID BARRETT
LEAD GUITAR

RICK WRIGHT
ORGAN

EMI RECORDS

Cordially invites you to a
SPECIAL COCKTAIL PARTY

To meet and hear the
MOST OUTSTANDING GROUP OF '67

THE PINK FLOYD

on FRIDAY MARCH 3rd 1967 at 12-30 pm

at EMI HOUSE
20 MANCHESTER SQUARE, LONDON, W.1

R.S.V.P.
COLIN BURN
EMI RECORDS
P.O. BOX 1ES
LONDON, W.1
Telephone HUNter 4488 ext: 471

Cocktails
refreshments

(public appearance only)

20 Jun Commemoration Ball, Magdalen College, Oxford, England

21 Jun Bolton College of Art Midsummer Ball, Rivington Hall Barn, Horwich, Bolton, England

23 Jun Rolls Royce Apprentice's Ball, The Locarno Ballroom, Derby, England

23 Jun 8-Hour Psycho-Chromatic Fantasy, Great & Small Halls, Bradford University, Bradford, England

24 Jun Civic Centre, Corby, England (cancelled)

24 Jun Cesars Club, Bedford, England (cancelled)

25 Jun Mister Smiths, Manchester, England (cancelled)

26 Jun Warwick University, Coventry, England

28 Jun The Ballroom, Eel Pie Island Hotel, Twickenham, England (cancelled)

30 Jun Bedford Park, London, England (unconfirmed)

1 Jul The Swan Public House, Yardley, Birmingham, England

2 Jul Digbeth Institute (Civic Hall), Digbeth, Birmingham, England

3 Jul The Pavilion, Bath, England

5 Jul The Ballroom, Eel Pie Island Hotel, Twickenham, England

6 Jul BBC Lime Grove Studios, Shepherds Bush, London, England (Top Of The Pops, BBC1 TV, live broadcast)

7 Jul The Birdcage Club, Eastney, Portsmouth, England

8 Jul Memorial Hall, Northwich, England

9 Jul Roundhouse, Chalk Farm, London, England (Late Night Line-Up, BBC2 TV)

13 Jul BBC Lime Grove Studios, Shepherds Bush, London, England (Top Of The Pops, BBC1 TV, live broadcast)

15 Jul Stowmarket Carnival, The Cricket Meadow, Stowmarket, England

16 Jul Redcar Jazz Club, Coatham Hotel, Redcar, England

17 Jul Rediffusion TV Studios, Wembley, England (Come Here Often, London Rediffusion London ITV Network TV, broadcast 18 Jul)

18 Jul The Palace Ballroom, Douglas, Isle of Man, England

19 Jul The Floral Hall, Gorleston, Norfolk, England

(Impresarios, BBC2 TV, broadcast 23 Oct)

20 Jul Two Red Shoes Ballroom, Elgin, Scotland

21 Jul Ballerina Ballroom, Nairn, Scotland

22 Jul The Beach Ballroom, Aberdeen, Scotland

23 Jul Cosmopolitan Ballroom, Carlisle, England

27 Jul BBC Lime Grove Studios, Shepherds Bush, London, England (Top Of The Pops, BBC1 TV, live broadcast)

28 Jul BBC Playhouse Theatre, Northumberland Ave., London, England (Saturday Club, BBC Radio 1, not broadcast)

28 Jul UFO, The Blarney Club, Tottenham Court Road, London, England

29 Jul Wellington Club, The Dereham Exchange, East Dereham, England

29 Jul Love In Festival, Alexandra Palace, Muswell Hill, London, England

31 Jul Town Hall, Torquay, England (rumoured to have been cancelled; a BD visitor states they saw the show)

1 Aug Music For Young People TV show, Hamburg, West Germany (cancelled)

2 Aug Music For Young People TV show, Hamburg, West Germany (cancelled)

5 Aug Seagull Ballroom, Ryde, Isle of Wight, England (cancelled)

10 Aug Skyline Ballroom, Hull, England (cancelled)

11 Aug Top Rank, Doncaster, England (cancelled)

12 Aug 7th NJF Festival, Royal Windsor Racecourse, Windsor, England (cancelled)

20 Aug Pavilion Ballroom, Hastings Pier, Hastings, England (cancelled)

1 Sep Gaiety (Mecca) Ballroom, Grimsby, England (cancelled)

1 Sep UFO Festival, Paignton, England (cancelled)

1 Sep UFO Festival, The Roundhouse, Chalk Farm, London, England

2 Sep UFO Festival, The Roundhouse, Chalk Farm, London, England

9 Sep Boom Dancing Center, Arhus, Denmark

10 Sep Gyllene Cirkeln, Stockholm, Sweden

ERIC BURDON
THE ANIMALS
PINK FLOYD
BRIAN AUGER
JULIE DRISCOLL AND THE TRINITY
CRAZY WORLD OF ARTHUR B
CREATION
TOMORROW
BLOSSOM TOES
LOVE IN FESTIVAL
ALEXANDRA PALACE
SATURDAY JULY 29
9PM TILL 9AM LONDON N22
SAM GOPAL DREAM
OVERHEAD LIGHTSHOW FLOWERS FOOD LIC. BAR
HAPPENIN
TICKETS £1.0.0 AVAILABLE AT KEITH PROWSE, ABBEY BOX LTD., CHALLICE & BENSON, BETTER BOOKS,
INDICA BOOKS, WAY IN, HAMPSTEAD RECORD CENTRE, MISS SELFRIDGE, MISS WARTSKI, TAKE 6, ALFRED HAYS LTD.

FROM ENGLAND
PINK FLOYD
LEE MICHAELS
CLEAR LIGHT
THURS-FRI-SAT
OCT. 26 27 28
FILLMORE
B. McLEAN
© BILL GRAHAM 1967
90

11 Sep Starclub, Copenhagen, Denmark
12 Sep Starclub, Copenhagen, Denmark
13 Sep Starclub, Copenhagen, Denmark
15 Sep Starlight Ballroom, Belfast, Northern Ireland
16 Sep Flamingo Ballroom, Ballymena, Ireland
17 Sep Arcadia Ballroom, Cork, Ireland
19 Sep Speakeasy Club, West End, London, England
21 Sep Assembly Hall, Worthing, England
22 Sep Tiles Club, Oxford Street, London, England
23 Sep Saturday Scene, Corn Exchange, Chelmsford, England
25 Sep BBC 201 Piccadilly Studios, London, England (Top Gear, BBC Radio 1, broadcast 1 Oct)
27 Sep Fifth Dimension, Leicester, England
28 Sep Skyline Ballroom, Hull, England
30 Sep Imperial Ballroom, Nelson, England
1 Oct Saville Theatre, Shaftesbury Avenue, London, England (two shows)
6 Oct Miss Teenage Brighton Contest, Top Rank Suite, Brighton, England
7 Oct Victoria Rooms, University of Bristol, Bristol, England
13 Oct The Pavilion, Weymouth, England
14 Oct Cesar's Club, Bedford, England
21 Oct Derwent Dining Room, University of York, Heslington, York, England
23 Oct The Pavilion, Bath, England (cancelled)
23 Oct Whisky A Go Go, West Hollywood, Los Angeles, CA, USA (cancelled)
24 Oct Whisky A Go Go, West Hollywood, Los Angeles, CA, USA (cancelled)
26 Oct Fillmore Auditorium, San Francisco, CA, USA (cancelled)
27 Oct Fillmore Auditorium, San Francisco, CA, USA (cancelled)
28 Oct Fillmore Auditorium, San Francisco, CA, USA (cancelled)
28 Oct Dunelm House, University of Durham, Durham, England
30 Oct KPFA Benefit, Fillmore Auditorium, San Francisco, CA, USA (cancelled)
30 Oct Whisky A Go Go, West Hollywood, Los Angeles, CA, USA (cancelled)
31 Oct Whisky A Go Go, West Hollywood, Los Angeles, CA, USA (cancelled)
1 Nov Whisky A Go Go, West Hollywood, Los Angeles, CA, USA (cancelled)
2 Nov Fillmore Auditorium, San Francisco, CA, USA (cancelled)
3 Nov Winterland Auditorium, San Francisco, CA, USA (cancelled)
3 Nov Caves Club, Chislehurst Caves, Chislehurst, England (cancelled)
4 Nov Winterland Auditorium, San Francisco, CA, USA
5 Nov Cheetah Club, Chicago, IL, USA (cancelled)
5 Nov Cheetah Club, Venice, Santa Monica, CA, USA (Groovy, KHJ Channel 9 TV, broadcast 16 Nov)
6 Nov KHJ TV Studios, Hollywood, Los Angeles, CA, USA (Pat Boone In Hollywood, KHJ Channel 9 TV, broadcast 4 Dec)
7 Nov Cafe Au Go Go, Manhattan, New York City, NY, USA (cancelled)
7 Nov ABC TV Studios, Burbank, Los Angeles, CA, USA (American Bandstand, ABC Channel 7 TV, broadcast 18 Nov)
8 Nov Cafe Au Go Go, Manhattan, New York City, NY, USA (cancelled)
8 Nov KHJ TV Studios, Hollywood, Los Angeles, CA (Boss City, KHJ Channel 9 TV, broadcast 11 Nov)
9 Nov Cafe Au Go Go, Manhattan, New York City, NY, USA (cancelled)
9 Nov Fillmore Auditorium, San Francisco, CA, USA
10 Nov Cafe Au Go Go, Manhattan, New York City, NY, USA (cancelled)
10 Nov Winterland, San Francisco, CA, USA
11 Nov Cafe Au Go Go, Manhattan, New York City, NY, USA (cancelled)
11 Nov Winterland, San Francisco, CA, USA
12 Nov Cafe Au Go Go, Manhattan, New York City, NY, USA (cancelled)
12 Nov Public Hall, Harpenden, England (cancelled)
13 Nov Hippy Happy Fair, De Oude-Ahoy Hallen, Ahoy

BILL GRAHAM PRESENTS IN SAN FRANCISCO
FILLMORE
NOV. 9
PROCOL HARUM
PINK FLOYD
H.P. LOVECRAFT
NOV. 10, 11
WINTERLAND
LIGHTS BY
HOLY SEE
NICHOLAS KOUNINOS
© BILL GRAHAM 1967 #92
TICKETS
SAN FRANCISCO: City Lights Bookstore; S.F. State College (Hut T-1); The Town Square (1318 Polk); Wild Colors
REDWOOD CITY: Redwood House of Music; PALO ALTO: Dana Morgan Music; SAN RAFAEL: Record King; SAUSALITO: The Tides.

Heliport, Rotterdam, The Netherlands

14 Nov The Alchemical Wedding, Royal Albert Hall, Kensington, London, England (Jimi Hendrix tour)

15 Nov Winter Gardens, Bournemouth, England (two shows; Jimi Hendrix tour)

17 Nov City (Oval) Hall, Sheffield, England (two shows; Jimi Hendrix tour)

17 Nov All Nite Garden Party, Queens Hall, Leeds, England

18 Nov Empire Theatre, Liverpool, England (two shows; Jimi Hendrix tour)

19 Nov Coventry Theatre, Coventry, England (two shows; Jimi Hendrix tour)

22 Nov Guildhall, Portsmouth, England (two shows; Jimi Hendrix tour)

23 Nov Sophia Gardens Pavilion, Cardiff, Wales (two shows; Jimi Hendrix tour)

24 Nov Colston Hall, Bristol, England (two shows; Jimi Hendrix tour)

25 Nov Opera House, Blackpool, England (two shows; Jimi Hendrix tour)

26 Nov Palace Theatre, Manchester, England (two shows; Jimi Hendrix tour)

27 Nov Festival '67, Whitla Hall, Queens College, Belfast, Northern Ireland (two shows; Jimi Hendrix tour; PF missed this show)

1 Dec Central Hall, Chatham, England (two shows; Jimi Hendrix tour)

2 Dec The Dome, Brighton, England (two shows; Jimi Hendrix tour)

3 Dec Theatre Royal, Nottingham, England (two shows; Jimi Hendrix tour)

4 Dec City Hall, Newcastle-Upon-Tyne, England (two shows; Jimi Hendrix tour)

5 Dec Green's Playhouse, Glasgow, Scotland (two shows; Jimi Hendrix tour)

6 Dec Horror Ball, Royal College of Art, Kensington, London, England

8 Dec Caves Club, Chislehurst Caves, Chislehurst, England

10 Dec Teenagers Sunday Club, The Birdcage, Harlow, England

13 Dec Flamingo Ballroom, Redruth, England

14 Dec Pavilion Ballroom, Bournemouth, England

15 Dec Middle Earth Club, Covent Garden, London, England

16 Dec Ritz Ballroom, Birmingham, England

16 Dec Saturday Spectacular, The Penthouse, Birmingham, England

20 Dec BBC Maida Vale Studios, London, England (Top Gear, BBC Radio 1, broadcast 31 Dec)

21 Dec Speakeasy Club, Margaret Street, London, England

22 Dec Christmas On Earth Continued, Olympia Exhibition Halls, Kensington, London, England

'I believe Syd was a casualty of the so-called "Psychedelic Period" that we were meant to represent. 'Cause everyone believed that we were taking acid before we went on stage and all that stuff. . . Unfortunately, one of us was and that was Syd.'

Roger Waters

In early 1967, 'Pink Floyd' began to attract the attention of the music industry. While in negotiations with record companies, UFO club manager Joe Boyd and the band's booking agent, Bryan Morrison arranged and funded a recording session at Sound Techniques studio in north London at the end of January. Within days, 'Pink Floyd' had signed with EMI who released the first single 'Arnold Layne' on March 10 1967. However, the references to cross-dressing led to a ban by several radio stations and the single peaked at number 20 in the charts. Their second single 'See Emily Play' was released three months later and reached number three while their first album 'The Piper at the Gates of Dawn', recorded in the late winter and spring of '67, was released that June in the UK and two months later in the US.

As for the shows? There were many, including the coolest event of the summer – The 14-Hour Technicolour Dream at Alexandra Palace in north London. And also, the ground-breaking 'Games for May' concert at the prestigious Queen Elizabeth Hall on London's South Bank. This was described as a '*Space age relaxation for the climax of spring – electronic composition, colour and image projection, girls, and the Pink Floyd*'. The show included a primitive surround sound mixer – the 'Azimuth Co-ordinator' – consisting of a joystick linked to an organ and effects, which could be used to move sounds around the auditorium by shifting phases between speakers. 'Games for May' was the first concert in Britain to feature both a complex light show and a quadraphonic sound system. The show was introduced with a series of recordings which Roger Waters had created from taping bird song and other natural sounds. The bubble sequence at the end of the show was created by Rick Wright while the ending piece was constructed by Barrett. During the performance, band members created sound effects by chopping up wood on stage and a man dressed up as an admiral gave out daffodils. But it would be the first and last time, 'Pink Floyd' would play at the venue. Rick Wright's bubbles stained the seating in the newly opened hall and as a consequence, they were banned from ever playing there again.

'We have only just started to scrape the surface of effects and ideas of lights and music combined,' Syd Barrett told music newspaper 'Melody Maker'.

Maybe so but Syd's behaviour – both on and off stage – was becoming noticeably erratic and increasingly disturbing.

'I remember I really started to get worried when I went

along to the recording session for "See Emily Play",' recalls Dave Gilmour. *'Syd was still functioning but he definitely wasn't the person I knew. He looked through you. He wasn't quite there. He was strange even then. That stare, you know?'*

On another occasion, Peter Jenner's PA, June Child – who would later marry Marc Bolan – found Syd totally out of it in UFO's dressing room when the band were due on stage.

'He was so. . .gone,' she said. *'Roger Waters and I got him on his feet, and we got him out to the stage ... The band started to play and Syd just stood there. He had his guitar around his neck and his arms just hanging down.'*

Syd was now taking copious amounts of LSD which hardly helped any underlying mental health issues he may have had and, as the year progressed, it was clear that he could no longer function as he had and many 'Pink Floyd' live shows were cancelled as a result. Forced to call off Pink Floyd's appearance at the prestigious National Jazz and Blues Festival, as well as several other shows, Andrew King informed the music press that Barrett was suffering from nervous exhaustion. Waters arranged a meeting with a psychiatrist and though he personally drove Barrett to the appointment, Barrett refused to come out of the car – just as he'd so often refuse to leave the tour bus when they had a gig. During 'Pink Floyd's' first tour of the US in October, Syd – and the tour itself – began to completely unravel. There were more cancellations and during appearances on the Dick Clark and Pat Boone shows, Barrett confounded his hosts by giving terse answers to questions or not responding at all. He refused to move his lips when it came to miming 'See Emily Play' on Boone's show.

'Syd went mad on that first American in the autumn of 1967,' remembers Nick Mason. *'He didn't know where he was most of the time. I remember he detuned his guitar on stage in Venice, Los Angeles, and he just stood there rattling the strings which was a bit weird, even for us.'*

After these embarrassing episodes, King ended the tour and immediately sent the band home to London. Soon after their return, they supported Jimi Hendrix during a tour of England. However, Barrett's mental health worsened as the tour continued. One occasions, when Barrett failed to turn up, the band were forced to replace him with singer/guitarist Davy O'List, borrowed from the opening band 'The Nice'. Barrett's condition had reached a crisis point, and the band responded by adding David Gilmour to their line-up, initially to cover for Syd's lapses during live performances.

'It was fairly obvious that I was brought in to take over from him, at least on stage,' says Gilmour. *'It was impossible to gauge his feelings about it – by that stage, I don't think Syd had opinions as such. The first plan was that I would join and make it a five-piece so it would make it easier – Syd could still be strange but the band would still function. And then the next idea was that Syd would stay home and do writing and be the Brian Wilson elusive character who didn't actually perform with us. The third plan was that he would do nothing at all. And it quickly changed round and it was just. . .it was obviously impossible to carry on working that way.'*

In the end Waters, Mason, Wright and now Gilmour came to realize that Syd was too unwell and too out of control to continue in any way and after playing five shows together as a five piece, they decided not to pick him up for the sixth gig. Syd Barrett played his last gig as a member of 'Pink Floyd' in January 1968.

'It wasn't impossible to play with Syd – it was totally impossible,' says Gilmour. *'It was a purely practical decision. There was no other choice left. If he'd stayed, the Floyd would have died an ignominious death.'*

FIRST WORLD TOUR

'David certainly wasn't perceived as the new boy'

Nick Mason

Although Syd Barrett exited 'Pink Floyd' in early 1968, it wasn't until April that his departure was formally announced. By then the band had new management in the form of the Brian Morrison Agency – Pete Jenner and Andrew King preferring to stick with Syd as they felt 'Pink Floyd' had no future without him. In February, the new-look band had embarked on a string of dates in Europe, kicking off on February 17 in the Netherlands. Most of Barrett's compositions were dropped from the set list and David Gilmour became the main frontman. However, Barrett's shoes were big to fill.

'It was very hard replacing one of my close friends,' said Gilmour, *'and having to see one of my close friends no longer function as a human being.'*

He did so with quiet professionalism – even when Syd turned up at one of their London 'Middle Earth' gigs *'one terrible night'* and relentlessly eye-balled his replacement from the front of the stage.

Life on the road, post Syd, was certainly calmer.

'This should have been a difficult time for us but we were about to enter a period I remember as being particularly happy,' recalled Nick Mason.

As in 1967, the tour schedule was relentless. But as the underground scene began to fragment combined with the band feeling they'd had their fill of 'Top Rank' type dates, a new kind of venue was emerging – the new universities springing up in Britain's major provincial cities – which happily welcomed bands like The Floyd to play at their Student Unions. In these venues, 'Pink Floyd' were greeted with respect – during some performances the audience would remain silent until the last note was played. However, logistically, the tour was – literally – all over the place.

'It wasn't touring but gigging,' says Nick Mason. *'There was no attempt to construct rational and logistically sensible journey cycles. We simply took any paying job and if that meant a gig near London followed by a one-off performance at the other end of the country before heading back to, say, Hull the following night, that was the way it was.'*

Europe was a success, giving the band time and space away from Britain to develop. They had never toured much on the continent with Syd so visiting the Low Countries, France and Italy was a positive experience for this new-look Floyd – even if they did get caught in the crossfire between warring student groups in Belgium at one concert and almost blinded by police letting off tear gas canisters in Italy at another. The reviews were certainly promising.

Pink Floyd shrouded in pink with new member Dave Gilmour, back right, August 1968

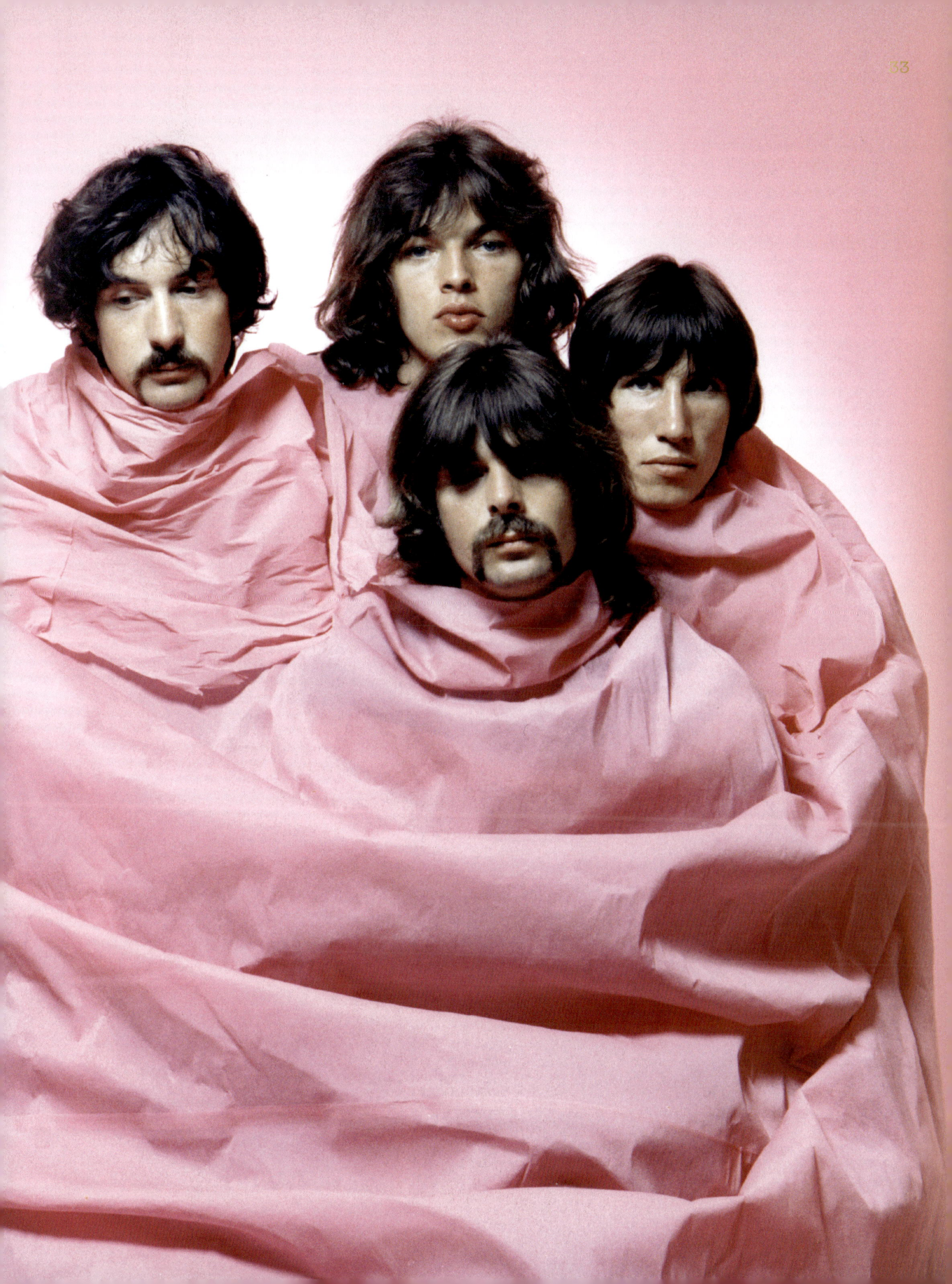

'Everything was perfectly enhanced by a primitive "sensual laboratory" that provided light and colour explosions all over the stage while keeping up with the devilish rhythms of the music, equalling a volcano-like outburst of sight and sound,' reported the Belgian 'Het Laatste Nieuws' about the gig in Antwerp in late February. *'The whole show was proof of a total communication through light and sound, a concept that left a beat-loving teenage audience stunned at first but in the end succeeded in drawing everyone into a whirlpool of music, sounds and multi-coloured light effects.'*

The band and crew were in harmony, few gigs were cancelled and equipment was still easily transportable. Their gear comprised of a stack of 4 x 4 speakers for Gilmour, Waters and Wright, with a four-channel mixer at the side of the stage feeding a couple of PA columns. The drums weren't miked up. Wright also had a Hammond organ by this point and it was the first outing for the famous gong which Waters relished striking. The Azimuth Co-ordinator was not featured. The light show was still mainly slide projectors with mounted spotlights and revolving daleks. With no Barrett manically moving around nor staring into space, the vibe was certainly more serene – apart from when Waters got going on the gong!

In between dates, Floyd recorded their second album – 'A Saucerful of Secrets'. Some tracks, penned by Barrett, had been laid down the previous year but only one – 'Jugband Blues' – made the final pressing. Roger Waters penned 'Let There Be More Light', 'Corporal Clegg' and 'Set the Controls for the Heart of the Sun'; Rick Wright wrote 'Remember a Day' and 'See Saw' while the title track was an ensemble piece written by all four band members. The album was released in the UK on June 28 – the day before 'Pink Floyd' played at the first free Hyde Park concert with Roy Harper, Tyrannosaurus Rex and Jethro Tull. DJ John Peel was, in the vernacular of the time, *'blown away'*! *'I always claim that the best outdoor event I've ever been to was the Pink Floyd concert in Hyde Park, when I hired a boat and rowed out and I lay in the bottom of the boat, in the middle of the Serpentine and just listened to the band play. I think their music then suited the open air perfectly. It was – it sounds ludicrous now, the kind of thing that you can get away with saying at the time and which now, in these harsher times, sounds a bit silly but I mean it was like a religious experience, it was that marvellous. They played "A Saucerful Of Secrets" and things. They just seemed to fill the whole sky and everything. And to coincide perfectly with the lapping of the water and the trees and everything. It just seemed to be the perfect event. I think it was the nicest concert I've ever been to.'*

To coincide with the US release of 'A Saucerful of Secrets' in July, the band headed to North America for the first time since their disastrous foray state-side the previous year. Things didn't get off to the best start as working visas were delayed which meant the band having to make a quick round trip to Canada while a lack of equipment proved problematic. Jimi Hendrix came to the rescue by sending them down to his 'Electric Lady' recording studio and storage facility in New York, and telling them to borrow whatever was required. Over six weeks, Floyd took in Chicago, Detroit, Philadelphia, New York, Seattle and Los Angeles, sharing stages with the likes of 'Santana', 'Fleetwood Mac' and 'The Stooges' – and receiving rave reviews.

'Pink Floyd overpowered a packed house at the Scene on Monday in a varied programme with a strong emphasis on space and oriental sounds,' wrote Billboard about one performance in New York. *'The inventiveness of "Pink Floyd" was remarkable. From the opening "Interstellar Overdrive" to the closing "A Saucerful of Secrets", the group displayed top-flight musicianship and consistent interest. An act that requires top effort from each member. "Pink Floyd" just drew that. The selection made the greatest use of church organ effect, however, in "Astronomy Domine". Gilmour's best vocal was "Flaming". But it was their inventiveness, musicianship and ability to say something musically whether playing and vocalising softly or overwhelming with cascades of sound.'*

Future 'Rolling Stone' writer David Fricke was equally impressed as he watched the band – a supporting act for 'The Who' at the 100,000 seater JFK stadium in Philadelphia.

Original vinyl album cover for Live In Amsterdam Fantasio Club

'From where I sat, the Floyd were tiny moving matchsticks,' he recalled. *'Yet the music was big enough to move the air. For the 40 minutes or so the Floyd were on stage they were the air.'*

Once back in the UK, Floyd resumed their usual routine of touring the British university circuits, interspersed with some European dates, including an outdoor show in Germany where students, inspired by the protests that had swept Europe and the US in 1968, decided that entry to the gig should be free and gate-crashed using a fleet of VW camper fans. The year ended on a high with a two-day event in the Netherlands with the band replacing Jimi Hendrix who had cancelled. It had been a challenging year – yet successful. What would 1969 bring?

1968

'I thought the new line-up was brilliant'

Jeff Dexter, DJ at Middle Earth club in London

Typical set list:

Keep Smiling PeopleLet There Be More LightSet the Controls for the Heart of the SunFlamingA Saucerful of SecretsCareful with That Axe, EugeneInterstellar OverdriveAstronomy Domine

17 Feb Concertgebouw, Vlissingen, The Netherlands
18 Feb RTB TV Studios, Brussels, Belgium (Vibrato, RTB TV, broadcast 27 Feb)
19 Feb RTB TV Studios, Brussels, Belgium (Tienerklanken, RTB TV, broadcast 31 Mar)
20 Feb ORTF TV Studios, Buttes Chaumont, Paris, France (Bouton Rouge, ORTF2 TV, broadcast 24 Feb)
21 Feb ORTF TV Studios, Buttes Chaumont, Paris, France (Discorama, ORTF2 TV, broadcast 17 Mar)
23 Feb Pannenhuis, Antwerp, Belgium
24 Feb Cheetah Club, Brussels, Belgium
26 Feb Domino Club, Lion Hotel, Cambridge, England
4 Mar Isleworth Film Studios, Isleworth, London, England (private party)
9 Mar Faculty of Technology Union, Manchester Technical College, Manchester, England
14 Mar Whitla Hall, Belfast, Ireland
15 Mar Stage Club, Clarendon Restaurant, Oxford, England
16 Mar Crawdaddy, Casino Hotel, Taggs Island, Hampton Court, England
16 Mar Middle Earth Club, Covent Garden, London, England
20 Mar New Grafton Rooms, Liverpool, England
22 Mar Sound Techniques Studios, Chelsea, London, England (sound recording for The Sound of Change, BBC2 TV, broadcast 10 Sep)
22 Mar Main Hall, Woolwich Polytechnic, Woolwich, London, England
24 Mar 11th Deutsches Frankfurt Jazz Festival, Volksbildungsheim, Frankfurt, West Germany (cancelled)
26 Mar Barnes Common, London, England (film recording for The Sound of Change, BBC2 TV, broadcast 10 Sep)
28 Mar Abbey Mills Pumping Station, East Stratford, London, England (All My Loving, BBC2 TV, broadcast 3 Nov)
11 Apr Studio 4, BBC TV Centre, White City, London, England (All My Loving, BBC2 TV, broadcast 3 Nov)
12 Apr RTB TV Studios, Brussels, Belgium
13 Apr RTB TV Studios, Brussels, Belgium
14 Apr RTB TV Studios, Brussels, Belgium
18 Apr Piper Club, Rome, Italy
19 Apr Piper Club, Rome, Italy
20 Apr Raven Club, RAF Waddington, England
30 Apr VARA TV Studios, Zaandam, The Netherlands (Moef Ga Ga, Nederland 2 TV, broadcast 1 May)
3 May Westfield College, Hampstead, London, England
5 May Theatre 140, Brussels, Belgium
6 May First European International Pop Festival, Palazzo dello Sport, EUR, Rome, Italy (Rome Goes Pop, BBC2 TV, broadcast 18 May)
11 May Brighton Arts Festival – The Gentle Sound of Light, Falmer House Courtyard, University of Sussex, Falmer, Brighton, England
17 May Middle Earth Club, Covent Garden, London, England
22 May Hotel Billard Palace, Antwerp, Belgium
23 May Whisky A Go Go, RK Verenigingsgebouw, Zaandam, The Netherlands
23 May Paradiso, Amsterdam, The Netherlands
25 May Mayfair Suite, The Belfry Hotel, Wishaw, Sutton Coldfield, Birmingham, England
26 May OZ Magazine benefit, Middle Earth Club, Covent Garden, London, England
31 May Paradiso, Amsterdam, The Netherlands
31 May Fantasio, Amsterdam, The Netherlands
1 Jun Lijn 3, Amsterdam, The Netherlands
1 Jun t'Smurf, De Engh, Bussum, The Netherlands
1 Jun Eurobeurs, Apeldoorn, The Netherlands
2 Jun Recta (Club '67), Ertvelde, Belgium
2 Jun Concertgebouw, Vlissingen, The Netherlands
3 Jun De Pas, Heesch, The Netherlands
3 Jun Parochieel Ontspannings Centrum, Weesp, The Netherlands
8 Jun Market Hall, Haverfordwest, Wales
12 Jun Architects Ball, Homerton College, Cambridge, England
12 Jun May Ball, Kings College, Cambridge, England

14 Jun	Midsummer Ball, University College London, Bloomsbury, London, England
21 Jun	Commemoration Ball, Balliol College, Oxford, England
21 Jun	Middle Earth Club, Covent Garden, London, England
21 Jun	The 1st Holiness Kitschgarten For The Liberation of Love & Peace in Colours, Houtrusthallen, Den Haag, The Netherlands
22 Jun	Lower Common Room, University of East Anglia, Norwich, England
25 Jun	BBC 201 Piccadilly Studios, London, England (Top Gear, broadcast 11 Aug & 8 Sep)
26 Jun	Sheffield Arts Festival, Lower Refectory, Sheffield University, Sheffield, England
28 Jun	Studio 7, BBC TV Centre, White City, London, England
28 Jun	Students Celebration Dance – The End Of It All Ball, Music Hall, Shrewsbury, England
29 Jun	Midsummer High Weekend, The Cockpit, Hyde Park, London, England
8 Jul	Kinetic Playground, Chicago, IL, USA
12 Jul	Grande Ballroom, Detroit, MI, USA
15 Jul	Steve Paul's The Scene, New York City, NY, USA
16 Jul	Steve Paul's The Scene, New York City, NY, USA
17 Jul	Steve Paul's The Scene, New York City, NY, USA
23 Jul	WKBS TV Studios, Philadelphia, PA, USA
24 Jul	Philadelphia Music Festival, JFK Stadium, Philadelphia, PA, USA
26 Jul	The Shrine Expo Hall, Los Angeles, CA, USA
27 Jul	The Shrine Expo Hall, Los Angeles, CA, USA
2 Aug	Avalon Ballroom, San Francisco, CA, USA
3 Aug	Avalon Ballroom, San Francisco, CA, USA
4 Aug	Avalon Ballroom, San Francisco, CA, USA
9 Aug	Eagles Auditorium, Seattle, WA, USA
10 Aug	Eagles Auditorium, Seattle, WA, USA
11 Aug	Eagles Auditorium, Seattle, WA, USA
16 Aug	Sound Factory, Sacramento, CA, USA
17 Aug	Sound Factory, Sacramento, CA, USA
23 Aug	The Bank, Torrance, CA, USA
24 Aug	The Bank, Torrance, CA, USA
31 Aug	Kastival '68 Festival, Kasterlee, Belgium
4 Sep	Middle Earth, The Clubhouse, Richmond Athletic Club, Richmond, England
6 Sep	ORTF TV Studios, Buttes Chaumont, Paris, France
7 Sep	Le Bilboquet, St Germain des Pres, Paris, France
13 Sep	Mothers, Erdington, Birmingham, England
14 Sep	First Fug Festivity, Westerkerk, Leeuwarden, The Netherlands (cancelled)
20 Sep	Victoria Rooms, University of Bristol, Clifton, Bristol, England
26 Sep	Mayfair Ballroom, Newcastle-upon-Tyne, England
27 Sep	Queens Hall, Dunoon, Scotland
29 Sep	The Maryland Ballroom, Glasgow, Scotland (unconfirmed)
4 Oct	Mothers, Erdington, Birmingham, England
6 Oct	The Country Club, Belsize Park, London, England
16 Oct	Theatre du Huitieme, Lyon, France
18 Oct	The Industrial Club, Norwich, England
19 Oct	Theatre 140, Brussels, Belgium
25 Oct	The Boat House, Kew, London, England
26 Oct	IC Hop, Imperial College, Kensington, London
26 Oct	Middle Earth, The Roundhouse, Chalk Farm, London, England
31 Oct	L'Antenne du Chapiteau du Kremlin-Bicetre, Val de Marne, Paris, France
2 Nov	London College of Printing, London, England
7 Nov	Porchester Hall, Bayswater, London, England
8 Nov	Fishmonger's Arms Public House, Wood Green, London, England
15 Nov	Blow Up Club, Munich, West Germany
16 Nov	Restaurant Olten-Hammer, Olten, Switzerland
16 Nov	Grosser Tanzparty, Coca-Cola Halle, Abtwil, Switzerland
17 Nov	2nd Pop & Rhythm and Blues Festival, Hazyland, Kongresshaus, Zurich, Switzerland
17 Nov	Spot Bar, Neuchâtel, Switzerland
22 Nov	Crawdaddy, The Club House, Richmond Athletic Club, Richmond, England

England

24 Nov The Country Club, Belsize Park, London, England

27 Nov The Student Union Building, University of Keele, Newcastle under Lyme, England

29 Nov Hanover Lodge, Bedford College, Regents Park, London, England

2 Dec Studio 4, BBC Maida Vale Studios, Maida Vale, London, England

5 Dec Bournemouth College Students Union Christmas

7 Dec Kaleidoscope '68, Liverpool Stadium, Liverpool, England

8 Dec ABC Cinema, Merthyr Tydfil, Glamorgan, Wales

12 Dec Christmas Revels Ball, College Of Art, Dundee, Scotland

13 Dec The New Marquee, Leeds, England

15 Dec City Hall, Newcastle-upon-Tyne, England

20 Dec BBC Paris Cinema, Lower Regent Street, London

27 Dec Grote Zaal, De Doelen, Rotterdam, The Netherlands

28 Dec Flight To Lowlands Paradise II, Margriethal-Jaarbeurs, Utrecht, The Netherlands

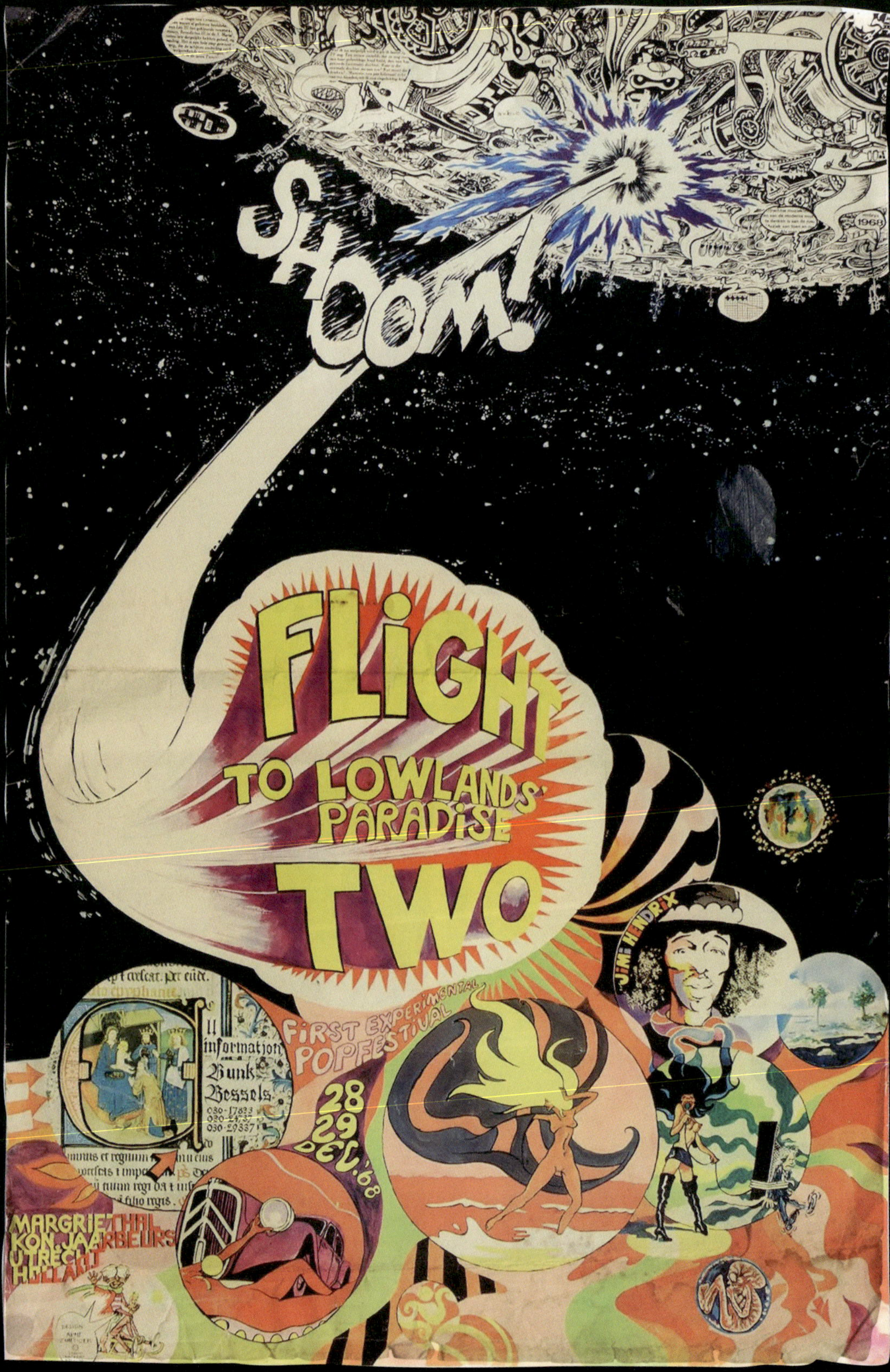
SHOOM!
FLIGHT
TO LOWLANDS' PARADISE
TWO
FIRST EXPERIMENTAL POPFESTIVAL
28 29 DEC. '68
JIMI HENDRIX
MARGRIETHAL
KON. JAARBEURS
UTRECHT
HOLLAND

BOYD GRAFMYRE AND KOL RADIO PRESENT:
AT EAGLE'S AUDITORIUM
JUNE 21, 22, 23
IRON BUTTERFLY
ATCO ARTISTS
JUNE 28 & 29
PAUL BUTTERFIELD BLUES BAND
ELECTRA ARTISTS
SPACE CONCERT
JULY 5 & 6
BLUE CHEER
PHILLIPS ARTISTS
JULY 12
THE DOORS
SEATTLE CENTER ARENA
ELECTRA ARTISTS
JULY 26 & 27
STEPPENWOLF
DUNHILL ARTISTS
"THE ORIGINAL" MOBY GRAPE
AUGUST 2 & 3
COLUMBIA ARTISTS
AUGUST 9 & 10
FROM ENGLAND
PINK FLOYD
Advanced tickets for eagles concerts available:
Discount Records in the U District
Warehouse of Music 5 & Pike
Bell, Book and Candle in Bellevue
Kern's Music & Farmer's Music in Burien
michael condon '68

'THE MAN' & 'THE JOURNEY'

'Floyd are an experience of the '60s and will still lead the way for progressive music into the '70s'

Liverpool Student Newspaper, November 1969

Ten days into 1969 and 'Pink Floyd' were back out on the road as their relentless gigging continued. Any traces of Syd Barrett's Floyd had – like the '67 summer of love – pretty much vanished, ditto the trippy light shows that had initially brought the band to attention. Now they were more concerned with wowing their audiences with their unique sound and stage craft rather than any kind of art-school, visual gimmickry. As in '68, their concerts were interspersed with TV appearances, radio recording sessions and an increasing amount of soundtrack work. They were commissioned by French film director Barbet Schroeder to score his movie 'More' and over five days in February 1969, entered the studio to record the soundtrack – the result of which would form much of their future set list.

Until April 1969 Floyd played similar venues to those performed in for the previous 12 months or so – 'Middle Earth', 'Top Rank Suites' in the provinces, university campuses – mostly sharing the bill with acts such as 'The Pretty Things', 'Spooky Tooth' and 'The Moody Blues' with a set list very similar to the 'Saucerful of Secrets' tour. Although certain 'performance art' elements were starting to creep into the show.

'A 65-minute set included the breaking of a milk bottle in a rubbish bin, the frying of eggs and gong-beating,' reported 'Time Out' about a January date at 'Middle Earth'.

Their performance at London's The Royal Festival Hall on April 14, marked something of a sea-change. The band premiered two new, conceptual suites of music – 'The Man' and 'The Journey' – in a show billed as 'The Massed Gadgets of Auximenes – More Furious Madness from Pink Floyd'.

'It was more than watching a band stand in front of 600 watts of Marshall speakers,' Rick Wright was later to say. *'It was about an entertaining show.'*

It was that – and then some. During 'The Man', taped sound effects, including Roger Waters screeching in a mock Scottish accent, *'If you don't eat your meat, you can't have your pudding'*, as well as the band's own performance, blasted around the venue courtesy of an updated version of the 'Azimuth Co-ordinator' sound machine. A wooden table was built on stage, around which the crew sat and drank tea while listening to a radio which was amplified through speakers. After which Rick Wright substituted his usual keyboards for a trombone. Other highlights included an alarm clock instrumental, an ethereal medley of keyboards, xylophone

Pink Floyd, 1969

and slide guitar, and, in 'Doing It', an homage to sex. In 'The Journey' section, the band went on a mystical trip – not the LSD version – incorporating music from the film 'More', a reworking of 'Careful of that Axe, Eugene' in the form of 'Beset By The Creatures of the Deep', taped recordings of footsteps echoing around the hall, and a stupendous finale of a three part sequence with Wright playing the Festival Hall Pipe Organ. Nick Mason was later to say it was one of the most memorable performances of his career.

'It was possibly less so for David, who courtesy of some bad earthing, received a bolt of electricity sufficient to hurl him across the stage and leave him vibrating mildly for the rest of the show. We'd decided to enhance the event with some performance art from our old Hornsey College of Art, friend Peter Dockley. Not only did he come up with the table construction idea but he also created a monster costume involving a gas mask and some enormous genitalia rigged up with a reservoir to enable him to "urinate" on the front row of the audience. This proved very effective indeed as during 'The Labyrinth', a gloomy, rather eerie piece of music, Peter crept around the audience while we used dripping sound effects in the quad system. One unfortunate girl, possibly under chemical influences, turned to find this horrific creature sitting next to her. She screamed and rushed from the auditorium never to be heard from again – not even from her lawyer.'

A month later, Floyd started their first headline tour playing, in many instances, to much larger audiences. In these larger venues, they would perform 'The Man' and 'The Journey'. So eagerly anticipated were these concerts that some venues even put out their own press releases beforehand.

'They plan to assault their unsuspecting audience by hurling music, lights, poetry and melodrama in furious succession,' read the release circulated by Fairfield Halls, Croydon. *'He who leaves the concert on steady feet will be constitutionally superhuman.'*

The most prestigious venue played was the majestic Royal Albert Hall in Kensington, London where, on June 26, Floyd performed their last concert of this short head-liner tour. Billed as 'The Final Lunacy', it was 'The Man' and 'The Journey' with extras! Rick Wright thundered away on the Hall's magnificent organ and the band were joined on stage by the brass section of London's Royal Philharmonic Orchestra and a choir. For the finale, two Waterloo cannons were fired and a huge pink smoke-bomb detonated – an action which went too far for the hall's management who promptly slapped a lifetime ban on Floyd. However, they were allowed back the year later.

Over the summer, the band worked on 'Ummagumma', their fourth release and a double album – one disc recorded in the studio, the other live.

'The first two sides captured our live sound at the time,' says Nick Mason, *'with a set – 'Astronomy', 'Careful with the Axe', 'Set the Controls' and 'Saucer' – recorded in June at Mothers in Birmingham (a kind of Midlands version of Middle Earth and a club we were very fond of) and Manchester College of Commerce.'*

A very enthusiastic John Peel was at the Mothers gig.

'At one moment they are laying surfaces of sound one upon another in symphonic thunder,' he wrote in 'Disc and Music Echo' magazine. *'At another isolated, incredibly melancholy sounds which cross one another sounding like cries of dying galaxies lost in sheer corridors of time and space.'*

Before the album was released in November, Floyd took to the road again, playing festivals in both Europe and the UK. Power cuts hampered the National Jazz and Blues Festival in August with delays meaning that many punters had fallen asleep by the time Floyd took to the stage. Then in September, heavy downpours of rain could have put a dampener on the Rugby Rag's Blues Festival which was policed peacefully by Hell's Angels but such was the band's performance and impressive lightshow, they were well received. Other highlights included

the four-day Actuel Festival in Belgium – billed as Europe's answer to Woodstock – that October where 'Pink Floyd' topped the bill on the second night. The stage was situated in a huge circus Big Top and compared by Frank Zappa who performed with many acts, including the Floyd, who treated the crowd to a 20-minute version of 'Interstellar Overdrive'.

In November 'Ummagumma' was released on November 7 1969 in the UK and a day later in the US. Reactions to the live disc were superior to those for the studio record, which as Roger Waters was later to say, hadn't been much of a team effort,

'I don't think it's a good idea to work in isolation,' he commented. *'I think what this demonstrates is that our sum is always better than our parts.'*

Album cover of Ummagumma by Pink Floyd released by Harvest Records in 1969

1969

‘Before a packed and rapturous audience, the Pink Floyd were a brilliant success with a two-and-a-half-hour programme of their unique brand of happening music’

Review in the Croydon Advertiser, May 1969

Typical set list for headline venues:

The Man SuiteDaybreak – aka Granchester Meadows WorkTeatime, AfternoonDoing ItSleepNightmareLabyrinth The Journey SuiteGreen is the ColourBeset by Creatures of the DeepThe Narrow WayThe Pink JungleThe Labyrinths of AuximenesBehold the Temple of LightThe End of the Beginning

10 Jan	Fishmonger's Arms Public House, Wood Green, London, England
12 Jan	Mothers, Erdington, Birmingham, England
18 Jan	Homerton College, Cambridge, England (unconfirmed)
18 Jan	Middle Earth, The Roundhouse, Chalk Farm, London, England (early hours 19 Jan)
22 Jan	ORTF Studios, Buttes Chaumont, Paris, France (Forum Musiques, ORTF1 TV, broadcast 15 Feb)
25 Jan	Sixty Nine Club, Royal York Hotel, Ryde, Isle of Wight, England
1 Feb	Winter Gardens, Malvern, England (unconfirmed)
12 Feb	Top Rank Suite, Cardiff, Wales
14 Feb	Valentines Ball, Edward Herbert Building, University of Loughborough, Loughborough, England
16 Feb	Students Union, St Andrews University, St Andrews, Scotland
17 Feb	The Ballroom, Bay Hotel, Whitburn, Sunderland, England
18 Feb	Manchester & Salford Students' Shrove Rag Ball, Manchester University, Manchester, England
21 Feb	Le Festival Sigma de Bordeaux, Alhambra Theatre, Bordeaux, France
24 Feb	The Dome, Brighton, England
25 Feb	Marlowe Theater, Canterbury, England
26 Feb	New Cavendish Ballroom, Edinburgh, Scotland
27 Feb	Glasgow Arts Lab Benefit, Maryland Ballroom, Glasgow, Scotland
28 Feb	Commemoration Ball, Queen Elizabeth College, Kensington, London, England
1 Mar	University College London, Bloomsbury, London, England
3 Mar	Vic Rooms Dance, Victoria Rooms, University Of Bristol, Clifton, Bristol, England
8 Mar	Reading University Rag Ball, New Union, Reading University, Reading, England
11 Mar	Lawns Centre, Cottingham, England
14 Mar	Van Dike Club, Devonport, Plymouth, England
15 Mar	Kee Club, Bridgend, Wales
19 Mar	Going Down Ball, The Refectory, University College, Swansea, Wales
20 Mar	Dunelm House, University of Durham, Durham, England
21 Mar	Blackpool Technical College & School of Art and St. Anne's College of Further Education Arts Ball, Empress Ballroom, Winter Gardens, Blackpool, England
22 Mar	Easter Endsville, Refectory Hall, University Union, Leeds University, Leeds, England
27 Mar	St. James' Church Hall, Chesterfield, England
14 Apr	Royal Festival Hall, London, England
19 Apr	SDR TV Villaberg TV Studios, Stuttgart, West Germany (Pink Floyd Mit Einen Neuen Beat Sound, SDR TV, pre-recorded broadcast)
23 Apr	NDR Radio Studios, Hamburg, West Germany (Psychedelic Sounds, pre-recorded radio broadcast)
26 Apr	Beat Club, Radio Bremen TV Studios, West Germany (Beat Club, pre-recorded TV broadcast)
26 Apr	Light & Sound Concert, Main Hall, Bromley Technical College, Bromley, England
27 Apr	Mothers, Erdington, Birmingham, England (Ummagumma recording)
2 May	Student Union Building, College of Commerce, Manchester, England (Ummagumma recording)
3 May	Sports Hall, Queen Mary College, Mile End, London, England
9 May	Camden Fringe Festival Free Concert, Parliament Hill Fields, Hampstead, London, England
9 May	Old Refectory, Student's Union, Southampton University, Southampton, England
10 May	Nottingham's Pop & Blues Festival, Notts County Football Ground, Nottingham, England
12 May	BBC Paris Cinema, Lower Regent Street, London (Top Gear, BBC Radio 1, broadcast 14 May)
15 May	It's A Drag – City of Coventry College of Art May Ball, Locarno Ballroom, Coventry, England
16 May	Town Hall, Leeds, England
24 May	City (Oval) Hall, Sheffield, England
25 May	A Benefit for Fairport Convention, The Roundhouse, Chalk Farm, London, England
29 May	HTV TV Studios, Bristol, England (Fusions, pre-recorded TV broadcast)
30 May	Fairfield Halls, Croydon, England
31 May	Eights Week Ball, Pembroke College, Oxford, England
8 Jun	Rex Ballroom, Cambridge, England
10 Jun	Ulster Hall, Belfast, Northern Ireland
13 Jun	Bradninch Dance, Great Hall, Devonshire House, University of Exeter, Exeter, England
14 Jun	Colston Hall, Bristol, England

15 Jun Guildhall, Portsmouth, England
16 Jun The Dome, Brighton, England
20 Jun Town Hall, Birmingham, England
21 Jun Royal Philharmonic, Liverpool, England
22 Jun Free Trade Hall, Manchester, England
24 Jun Commemoration Ball, Queens College, Oxford, England
26 Jun The Final Lunacy, Royal Albert Hall, Kensington, London, England
28 Jun Saturday Dance Date, Winter Gardens Pavillion, Weston-Super-Mare, England
30 Jun President's Ball, Top Rank Suite, Cardiff, Wales
4 Jul Selby Festival, James Street Recreation Ground, Selby, England
20 Jul Studio 5, BBC TV Centre, Wood Lane, London, England (So What If It's Just Green Cheese?, BBC1 TV, live broadcast)
22 Jul SDR TV Villa Berg Studios, Stuttgart, West Germany (P1, SDR TV, broadcast 21 Sep)
23 Jul TV show, West Germany
24 Jul VARA TV Studios, Zaandam, The Netherlands (Een Man op de Maan, Nederland1 TV, live broadcast)
24 Jul ARD TV Studios, Hamburg, West Germany (Apollo 11, pre-recorded TV broadcast)
1 Aug Van Dike Club, Devonport, Plymouth, England
8 Aug 9th National Jazz Pop Ballads & Blues Festival, Plumpton Racecourse, Plumpton, England
13 Sep Sam Cutler Stage Show, Rainsbrook, Ashlawn Road, Rugby, England
17 Sep Concertgebouw, Amsterdam, The Netherlands (Hilversum 3 radio, broadcast late 1969)
19 Sep Grote Zaal, De Doelen, Rotterdam, The Netherlands
20 Sep Concertzaal de Jong, Groningen, The Netherlands
21 Sep Het Kolpinghuis, Nijmegen, The Netherlands
21 Sep Tiel, The Netherlands
22 Sep BRT TV Studios, Brussels, Belgium
23 Sep BRT TV Studios, Brussels, Belgium
24 Sep Stadgehoorzaal, Leiden, The Netherlands
25 Sep Staargebouw, Maastricht, The Netherlands
26 Sep Theatre 140, Brussels, Belgium
27 Sep Theatre 140, Brussels, Belgium
28 Sep Theatre 140, Brussels, Belgium
3 Oct Debating Hall, Birmingham University, Edgbaston, Birmingham, England
4 Oct New Union, Reading University, Reading, England
10 Oct Edward Herbert Building, University of Loughborough, Loughborough, England
11 Oct Internationales Essener Pop & Blues Festival '69, Gruga Halle, Essen, West Germany
18 Oct University College London, Bloomsbury, London, England
24 Oct Fillmore North, Locarno Ballroom, Sunderland, England
25 Oct Actuel Festival, Kluisbergbos, near Amougies, Belgium
27 Oct Electric Garden, Glasgow, Scotland
1 Nov Main Debating Hall, Manchester University, Manchester, England
2 Nov London College of Printing, London, England
7 Nov Main Hall, Waltham Forest Technical College, Walthamstow, London, England
26 Nov Friars Club, Queensway Hall, Civic Center, Dunstable, England
27 Nov Mountford Hall, Liverpool University, Liverpool, England
28 Nov Brunel University Arts Festival Weekend, Refectory Hall, Brunel University, Uxbridge, England
30 Nov The Lyceum, Strand, London, England
6 Dec Afan Festival of Progressive Music, Afan Lido Indoor Sports Centre, Port Talbot, Wales

MOTHERS
PINK FLOYD
SUN 27 APR
ERDINGTON

TOWN HALL LEEDS
FRIDAY, MAY 16th 8.15p.m.
the massed gadgets
of auximines
Pink floyd
in
stereo concert
with the
'azimuth co-ordinator'
TICKETS 15/- 12/6 10/- 8/6 6/6
from BARKERS, 91 THE HEADROW, LEEDS, 1
Tele. 33099

MALVERN
WINTER · GARDENS
PINK
FLOYD
ROY GEE+
STAX MOVEMENT
SAT. 1st FEB
8~11·30, 10/-
COMPERE · DAVE · MUNROE

ELECTRIC GARDEN
goes
UNDERGROUND
EVERY MONDAY NIGHT!
Starting MONDAY, 27 OCTOBER with
PINK FLOYD
supported by the STOICS
ADM. 10s
advance tickets from Electric Garden
and CUTHBERTSON'S, Cambridge Street
DOORS OPEN
7·30 pm

D.T.C. STUDENTS UNION
PRESENTS
the PINK FLOYD
also
DOCTOR K's BLUES BAND
THURSDAY MARCH 20th. at
DUNELM HOUSE
8·15P.M. to 1·30A.M.
ADMISSION 12/6
LICENSED UNTIL 12·30
TICKETS AVAILABLE FROM THE STUDENTS UNION
TELEPHONE DURHAM 5900

A NEW DECADE

'The volume on a couple of their disturbing, destructive numbers was quite terrifying – enough to make you feel physically ill'

The Bristol Evening Post, March 1970

In January 1970, Pink Floyd began a 16-date UK and French tour, commencing at the University of Nottingham and concluding at Leeds University in late February. The tour also took in two gigs in Paris. The set list included an early version of the piece later known as 'Atom Heart Mother', then an untitled instrumental piece which would eventually become the title of their next album. At this stage, it was known by the band as 'The Amazing Pudding' – which would later become the title of a Floyd fanzine. On completing these dates, Floyd took time off the road to go into the studio to begin recording 'Atom Heart Mother'. Within days, they were touring again – a handful of British gigs before embarking on a short tour of northern Europe, culminating in an appearance at the much-hyped but shambolically organised 'Le Festival Musique Evolution' over the Easter weekend in Paris. April saw them arriving in the US for an 18 -date tour – their first foray across 'the pond' since 1968. However, unlike that outing when equipment had been in short supply, necessitating a 'lend' from Hendrix, Floyd were now utilising a massive three tonnes of kit on stage.

'Their sound system is beyond belief,' Underground publication 'Great Speckled Brief' reported about one of their Stateside dates. *'But they are perhaps one of the few groups that know how to properly use their sound equipment.'*

The tour ended abruptly in New Orleans on May 16 after their 30-foot truck containing $40,000 worth of equipment was stolen from outside the hotel where they were staying. The stolen truck was found but Floyd decided against resuming the tour, preferring to head back to the studio in the UK to continue work on the album.
The official live rendition of the Atom Heart Mother phenomenon was unveiled when they headlined the second night of the 'Bath Festival Of Blues & Progressive Music'. Their late-night set included material from 'Atom Heart Mother', with the band attempting to emulate on stage the elaborate creation they'd laid down in the studio – complete with choir and brass section, one member of whom accidently emptied a pint of beer into their tuba before the performance began. However, this did little to dampen the reaction of the audience – or the critics.

'It was a heavenly sound,' enthused 'Disc & Music Echo'. *'The finale saw three flares bursting open the sky with a galaxy of colours – smoke and the light show flooded the stage. It was amazing.'*

The next night, the extravaganza – minus the orchestra on this occasion – was repeated to an enthralled 350,000 strong crowd at a festival in the Netherlands – even though, due to delays, Floyd didn't appear on stage until 4am! On July 18, Floyd returned to Hyde Park in London where they headlined free concert 'Blackhill's Garden Party', organised, as in 1969, by their former managers Peter Jenner and Andrew King. Here, they were joined on stage by choir and brass section for the 25-minute 'Atom Heart Mother' finale.

Singer, songwriter and composer Roger Waters of Pink Floyd, circa 1970

From late July, the band, crew and their friends and families rented a villa in St Tropez, France, for was anticipated would be a working holiday playing at a series of French festivals. However, only a handful of these materialised due to civil unrest in the area. Then, just before 'Atom Heart Mother' was released in early October, they took off to the US for the second time that year for a month-long tour. Within a week of arriving back in the UK, they were touring Europe again. Performing such an opus as 'Atom' live on stage in different venues and countries was, according to David Gilmour, problematic.

'Something on the scale of "Atom Heart Mother" really takes a lot of getting together. The problem is that we've never done it more than once with the same people. The choir is usually all right because they're used to working together but some of the brass people have been really hopeless. We had problems with the sound equipment, getting it mic'ed up and balanced and stuff. The trouble was not having enough rehearsal time everywhere we did it, because we used a different brass and choir group in Europe than we did on the East Coast of the US, and another on the West Coast. So, we used three completely different sets of people performing it.'

Pink Floyd gig on 16th June 1971 at the Abbey of Royaumont

Floyd concluded the year by going on six-date tour of the UK in December. Highlights included choir and brass sections joining them on stage for four of the dates, tea-making and egg-and-bacon frying carried out on stage, a tongue-in-cheek reference to BBC DJ Jimmy Young who had slated the band and Nick Mason dressing up as Santa Claus. It had been an eventful – and exhausting – year.

'Although we wanted the workload, we were probably unaware how exhausting it all was,' Mason was later to say. *'But at the start of 1971, we turned our attention – and any energies we did have – to our next album which we started at EMI in January.'*

Energies may have been concentrated on recording their sixth album but just a few weeks into 1971, Floyd were undertaking a five-date tour of the UK university circuit, beginning at Leeds University and ending at Queen Mary College, Twickenham. This was swiftly followed by a European tour, commencing at Halle Munsterland, Munster, West Germany – although the second half of this concert was almost cancelled when the band discovered that the musical score for Atom Heart Mother, required by the brass section, had been left behind in London. A courier was hastily dispatched to Dusseldorf and a police car raced from the airport to the venue, arriving at 10.30pm.

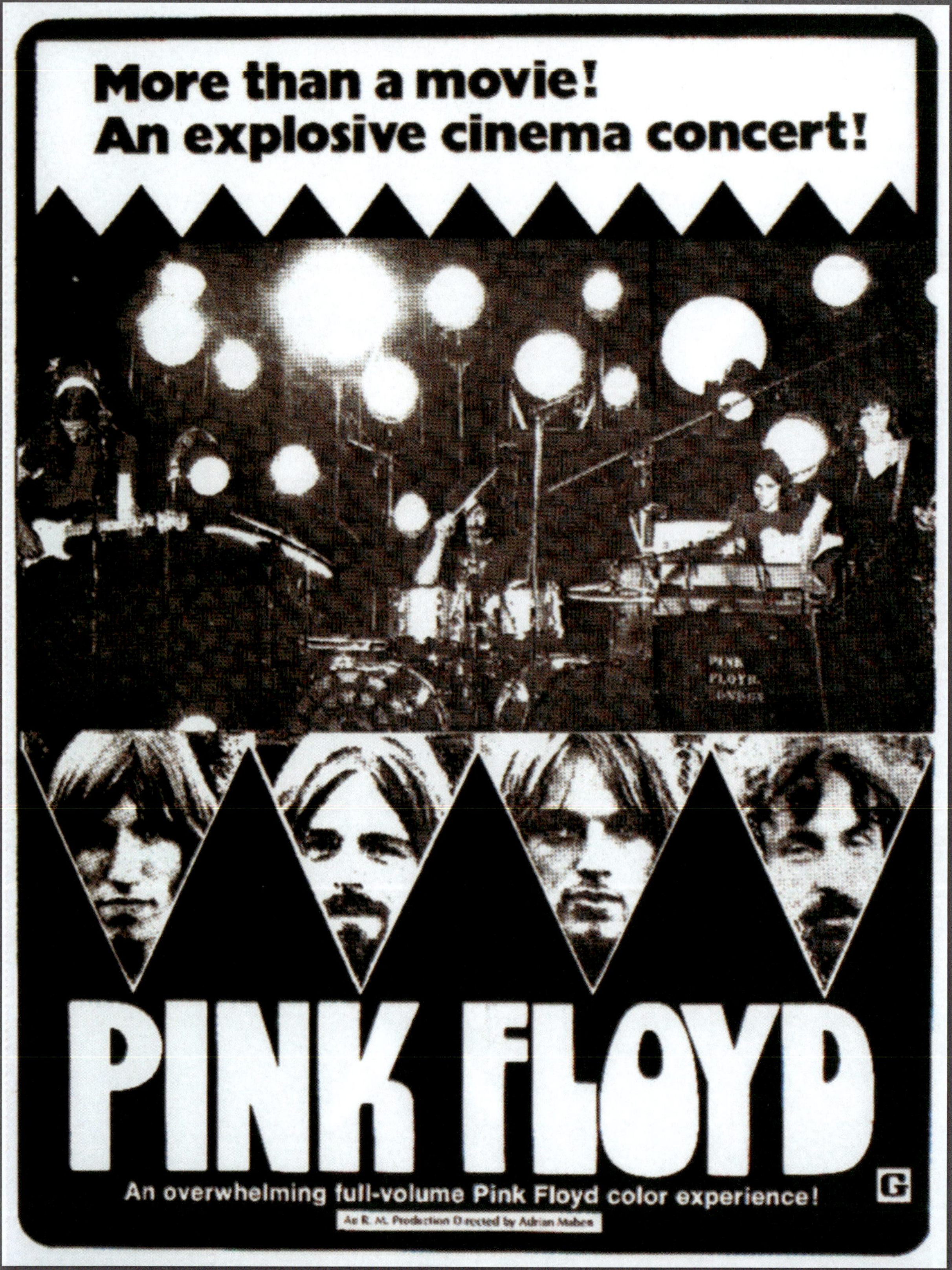
More than a movie!
An explosive cinema concert!
PINK FLOYD
G
An overwhelming full-volume Pink Floyd color experience!
An R. M. Production Directed by Adrian Maben

In May 1971, compilation album 'Relics' – *'a bizarre collection of antiques and curios'* as it was dubbed – while sixth album 'Meddle' was in gestation. Shortly afterwards, Floyd headined 'The Garden Party' at London's Crystal Palace Bowl, playing to an audience of 15,000. The band's party-piece, show-stopper included the appearance of a large inflatable octopus in the lake in front of the stage. As with previous larger-than-life, live shows, old friend Peter Dockery had been employed to work some of his art installation magic. It all started to go wrong when the octopus was due to emerge. They intended to blow it up with underwater smoke flares. Unfortunately, overeager concertgoers wading around the water caused the octopus to develop several tears. These caused smoke to escape into the pond instead of filling the octopus. To make matters worse, the band had also dumped a ton of dry ice, orange smoke bombs, and fireworks into the pond mechanism for added psychedelic effects. The combination of these, likely poisoned and suffocated the real-life marine life in the pond. An added blow was the impact of Floyd's patented quadraphonic sound system — a wall of surround sound placed around the outdoor venue. This sent massive sound waves through the earth toward the pond. Sound was everywhere, it was loud, a shock to everyone and everything. The vibrations coming off the stage likely killed any remaining fish struggling to breathe in the smoke-filled water. It may have even killed the water lilies. The band later received a bill from the council to repay the cost of the thousands of dead fish and restore marine life to the garden.

A scheduled appearance at the first 'Glastonbury' in June 1971 failed to take place because the band's equipment was delayed in Europe before they jetted off to Japan for their first tour of the Land of the Rising Sun at the end of July. Comprising of just three dates – two days at a festival and one at the Festival Hall in Osaka, it was deemed a success. *'Of all the overseas tours, our first visit to Japan was a particular success,'* recalled Nick Mason. *'The record company organised a press conference (something which we generally hate) and presented us with our first gold records. Although these were completely bogus, as they had not been earned through sales, we nonetheless appreciated the gesture.'*

Their first visit to Australia was a bit of a let-down in comparison. They played just two dates – one in Melbourne and the other in Sydney – but reviews were hardly glowing.

'Pink Floyd are very serious as they play,' noted Go-Set magazine's reviewer. *'The only showmanship is that of concentration.'*

The band concurred. . .

'In the '70s people came to hear the music,' Rick Wright was later to say. *'They didn't come to see me, Dave and Roger jumping around as individuals. We weren't standard rock n' roll people desperate to be personalities. We were happy not to be in the limelight.*

By early September 1971, Floyd were back in the studio, putting their finishing touches to 'Meddle', their most complex album to date which used household objects as a theme and as percussion instruments. A month later, they began four days of filming at the Roman amphitheatre in Pompeii, Italy. The film, directed by Adrian Maben, and eventually titled 'Pink Floyd: Live at Pompeii', went on general release in the UK in 1972. Mid-October saw them begin a 27-date North American tour at San Francisco's Winterland Auditorium, ending at Cincinnati Ohio's Taft Auditorium. It was their longest tour of the US and Canada to date and saw them performing material from 'Meddle', which was released on October 30 in the US and on November 5 in the UK. Reviews of the tour were mixed. One journalist found the gig at the prestigious Princetown University to be so loud, he walked out half way through, while another reviewer dismissed the performance of their new 'Echoes' epic as *'pure electronic garbage'*. This tour would mark the last time 'Echoes' was played live.

1970

'We were working on a very long, rather majestic but quite unfocused and still unfinished piece – one way to develop such a piece was to play it live so we played shortened versions at a number of gigs'

Nick Mason on the Atom Heart Mother concept

10 Jan The Ballroom, University of Nottingham, Beeston, Nottingham, England
17 Jan Lawns Centre, Cottingham, Hull, England
18 Jan Fairfield Hall, Croydon, England
19 Jan The Dome, Brighton, England
23 Jan Civic Hall, Wolverhampton, England (cancelled)
23 Jan Theatre des Champs-Elysées, Elysée, Paris, France (broadcast on Europe 1 Radio)
24 Jan Theatre des Champs-Elysées, Elysée, Paris, France
2 Feb Palais des Sports, Lyon, France
5 Feb Cardiff Arts Centre Project Benefit Concert, Sophia Gardens Pavilion, Cardiff, Wales
7 Feb Royal Albert Hall, Kensington, London, England
8 Feb Opera House, Manchester, England
11 Feb Town Hall, Birmingham, England
14 Feb King's Hall, Town Hall, Stoke-On-Trent, England
15 Feb Empire Theatre, Liverpool, England
17 Feb City Hall, Newcastle-upon-Tyne, England
22 Feb The Electric Garden, Glasgow, Scotland
24 Feb SB/DG BBC Maida Vale Studios, Maida Vale, London, England (Top Gear, BBC Radio 1, broadcast 14 Mar)
28 Feb Endsville '70, Refectory Hall, University Union, Leeds University, Leeds, England
5 Mar Studio B, BBC TV Centre, White City, London, England (Line Up, BBC1 TV, broadcast 13 Mar)
6 Mar Great Hall, College Block, Imperial College, London, England
7 Mar University of Bristol Arts Festival – Timespace, Colston Hall, Bristol, England
8 Mar Mothers, Erdington, Birmingham, England
9 Mar City (Oval) Hall, Sheffield, England
11 Mar Stadthalle, Offenbach, West Germany
12 Mar Kleiner Saal, Auditorium Maximum, Hamburg University, Hamburg, West Germany
13 Mar Konzert Saal, Technische Universität, West Berlin, West Germany (two shows)
14 Mar Grosser Saal, Meistersinger Halle, Nuremberg, West Germany

Typical 1970/71 set list:

EmbryoGreen is the ColourCareful with that Axe, EugeneCymablineSet the Controls for the Heart of the SunAtom Heart MotherA Saucerful of SecretsEchoes

15 Mar	Niedersachsenhalle, Hannover, West Germany
18 Mar	Gothenberg, Sweden (cancelled)
19 Mar	Stora Salen, Stockholm Konserthus, Stockholm, Sweden
20 Mar	Akademiska Foreningens Stora Sal, Lund, Sweden
21 Mar	Tivolis Koncertsal, Copenhagen, Denmark
30 Mar	Le Festival Musique Evolution, Le Bourget, Aeroport de Paris, Siene St Denis, France
9 Apr	Fillmore East, Manhattan, New York City, NY, USA
10 Apr	Aragon Ballroom, Chicago, IL, USA
11 Apr	The Gymnasium, State University of New York, Stony Brook, Long Island, NY, USA
12 Apr	Boston Tea Party, Boston, MA, USA
16 Apr	Fillmore East, Manhattan, New York City, NY, USA
17 Apr	Electric Factory, Philadelphia, PA, USA (two shows)
18 Apr	Electric Factory, Philadelphia, PA, USA (two shows)
22 Apr	Capitol Theater, Port Chester, NY, USA
24 Apr	Eastown Theater, Detroit, MI, USA
25 Apr	Eastown Theater, Detroit, MI, USA
28 Apr	Fillmore, San Francisco, CA, USA (PBS Network TV, live recording, no audience, broadcast 26 Jan 1971)
28 Apr	Pritchard Auditorium, San Francisco, CA, USA
29 Apr	Fillmore West, San Francisco, CA, USA
1 May	Civic Auditorium, Santa Monica, CA, USA
? May	University of California Los Angeles, West Hollywood, Los Angeles, CA, USA
9 May	San Diego, CA, USA (cancelled)
9 May	Terrace Ballroom, Salt Lake City, UT, USA
12 May	Municipal Auditorium, Atlanta, GA, USA
15 May	The Warehouse, New Orleans, LA, USA
16 May	The Warehouse, New Orleans, LA, USA
22 May	Houston Music Theatre, Houston, TX, USA (cancelled)
23 May	State Fair Music Hall, Dallas, TX, USA (cancelled)
24 May	Kansas City, MO, USA (cancelled)
29 May	Aragon Ballroom, Chicago, IL, USA (rescheduled to 10 Apr)
30 May	Aragon Ballroom, Chicago, IL, USA

(rescheduled to 10 Apr)

5 Jun Ludlow Garage, Cincinnati, OH, USA (cancelled)

5 Jun Ludlow Garage, Cincinnati, OH, USA (cancelled)

5 Jun SB/DG Extravaganza '70 Music & Fashion Festival, Olympia Exhibition Hall, Kensington, London, England

27 Jun Bath Festival of Blues & Progressive Music '70, Bath & West Showground, Shepton Mallet, England (with orchestra and choir)

28 Jun Holland Pop Festival, Kralingse Bos, Rotterdam, The Netherlands (Stamping Ground, film)

2 Jul 1st Open Air Pop Festival, Reiterstadion Soers, Aachen, West Germany

6 Jul BBC Paris Cinema, Lower Regent Street, London, England (Peel Sunday Concert, BBC Radio 1, broadcast 19 Jul) (with orchestra and choir)

8 Jul Blackhill's Garden Party – Hyde Park Free Concert, Hyde Park, London, England (with orchestra and choir)

26 Jul XI Festival International de Jazz, Pinède Gould, Antibes Juan-les-Pins, France

30 Jul VPRO Pik Nik Festival, Gemeendecentrum, Drijbergen, The Netherlands (cancelled)

1 Aug Festival d'Aix-en-Provence, Parc de Saint Pons, Aix-en-Provence, France (cancelled)

5 Aug Popanalia Festival, Autoroute De L'Esteral, Biot,

8 Aug Pop Festival Saint Raphael, Stade Municipal, St. Raphaël, France (cancelled)

8 Aug Festival de St. Tropez, Route Des Salins, San Tropez, France (Pop 2, ORTF 2 TV, broadcast 10 & 24 Oct)

12 Aug Fête de St. Raphaël, L'Amphithéâtre Romain, Fréjus, St. Raphaël, France

15 Aug Yorkshire Folk, Blues & Jazz Festival, Krumlin, Barkisland, Halifax, England (cancelled)

29 Aug Open Air Festival Heidelberg, Thingstätte Amphitheatre, Heidelberg, West Germany (cancelled)

31 Aug Charlton Park, Bishopsbourne, near Canterbury, England

12 Sep Fete de L'Humanite, Grand Scene, Bois de Vincennes, Paris, France (filmed, not broadcast) (with orchestra and choir)

26 Sep The Electric Factory, Philadelphia, PA, USA

27 Sep Fillmore East, Manhattan, New York City, NY, USA (two shows)

1 Oct Memorial Coliseum, Portland, OR, USA

2 Oct The Gymnasium, Gonzaga University, Spokane, WA, USA (rescheduled to 4 Oct)

2 Oct Moore Theater, Seattle, WA, USA

3 Oct Moore Theater, Seattle, WA, USA

4 Oct Open House, Seattle, WA, USA (rescheduled to 2 & 3 Oct)

6 Oct Central Washington University, Ellensburg, WA, USA
7 Oct Gardens Arena, Vancouver, B.C., Canada
8 Oct Jubilee Auditorium, Calgary, Alberta, Canada
9 Oct Sales Pavilion Annex, Edmonton, Alberta, Canada
10 Oct The Gardens, Edmonton, Alberta, Canada (rescheduled to 9 Oct)
10 Oct Centennial Auditorium, Saskatoon, Saskatchewan, Canada
11 Oct Centre of the Arts, Regina, Saskatchewan, Canada
13 Oct Centennial Concert Hall, Winnipeg, Manitoba, Canada
15 Oct Terrace Ballroom, Salt Lake City, UT, USA
16 Oct Pepperland Auditorium, San Rafael, CA, USA
17 Oct Pepperland Auditorium, San Rafael, CA, USA
18 Oct Intercollegiate Baseball Facility, University of California, San Diego, CA, USA
21 Oct Fillmore West, San Francisco, CA, USA (with orchestra and choir)
23 Oct Civic Auditorium, Santa Monica, CA, USA (with orchestra and choir)
25 Oct Boston Tea Party, Boston, MA, USA
31 Oct Black Magic & Rock & Roll, Cincinnati Gardens, Cincinnati, OH, USA (cancelled)
6 Nov Concertgebouw, Amsterdam, The Netherlands
7 Nov Grote Zaal, De Doelen, Rotterdam, The Netherlands
11 Nov Konserthuset, Gothenburg, Sweden
12 Nov Falkoner Teater, Copenhagen, Denmark (two shows)
13 Nov Vejlby Risskov Hallen, Arhus, Denmark
14 Nov Ernst-Merck Halle, Hamburg, West Germany
19 Nov Civic Arena, Pittsburgh, PA, USA (rescheduled to Syria Mosque)
21 Nov Super Pop '70 VII, Casino de Montreaux, Altes Casino, Montreux, Switzerland
22 Nov Super Pop '70 VII, Casino de Montreaux, Altes Casino, Montreux, Switzerland
23 Nov Grosser Konzerthaussaal, Wiener Konzerthaus, Vienna, Austria (rescheduled to 29 Nov)
25 Nov Friedrich Ebert Halle, Ludwigshafen, West Germany
26 Nov Killesberg Halle 14, Stuttgart, West Germany
27 Nov Neidersachsenhalle, Hannover, West Germany
28 Nov Saarlandhalle, Saarbrucken, West Germany
29 Nov Grosser Konzerthaussaal, Wiener Konzerthaus, Vienna, Austria (cancelled)
29 Nov Circus Krone, Munich, West Germany
5 Dec ORTF TV Studios, Buttes Chaumont, Paris, France (Volumes, ORTF2, broadcast 27 May 1971)
11 Dec Big Apple, Regent Theatre, Brighton, England
12 Dec The Roundhouse Public House, Dagenham, England
18 Dec Town Hall, Birmingham, England (with orchestra and choir)
20 Dec Colston Hall, Bristol, England (with orchestra and choir)
21 Dec Free Trade Hall, Manchester, England (with orchestra and choir)
22 Dec City (Oval) Hall, Sheffield, England (with orchestra and choir)

1971

17 Jan Implosion, The Roundhouse, Chalk Farm, London, England (with orchestra and choir)

23 Jan Refectory Hall, University Union, Leeds University, Leeds, England

3 Feb Great Hall, Devonshire House, University of Exeter, Exeter, England

12 Feb Lecture Theatre Block 6 & 7, University of Essex, Wivenhoe Park, Colchester, England

13 Feb Student Union Bar, Farnborough Technical College, Farnborough, England

16 Feb BBC Transcription Services Studios, Shepherds Bush, London, England

20 Feb The Theatre, St. Mary's College, Strawberry Hill, Twickenham, London, England

24 Feb Halle Munsterland, Munster, West Germany (with orchestra and choir)

25 Feb Grosser Saal, Musikhalle, Hamburg, West Germany (with orchestra and choir)

26 Feb Stadthalle, Offenbach, West Germany (with orchestra and choir)

27 Feb ORTF TV Studios, Buttes Chaumont, Paris, France

3 Apr Sportpaleis Ahoy, Rotterdam, Netherlands (with orchestra and choir)

16 Apr Top Rank Suite, Doncaster, England

22 Apr Norwich Lads Club, Norwich, England

7 May Central Hall, University of Lancaster, Bailrigg, Lancaster, England

15 May Crystal Palace Garden Party, Crystal Palace Bowl, Crystal Palace, London, England

18 May Pathfoot Building Refectory, University of Stirling, Stirling, Scotland

19 May Students' Centre Refectory, Edinburgh University, Scotland

20 May	The Ballroom, University of Strathclyde, Glasgow, Scotland
21 May	Students Union, Trent Polytechnic, Nottingham, England
4 Jun	Philipshalle, Dusseldorf, West Germany
5 Jun	Berliner Sportpalast, West Berlin, West Germany
12 Jun	Palais des Sports, Lyon, France) (with orchestra and choir)
15 Jun	Le Cloître, Abbaye de Royaumont, Asnières-sur-Oise, France
19 Jun	Palazzo delle Manifestazioni Artistiche, Brescia, Italy
20 Jun	Palaeur dello Sport EUR, Rome, Italy
23 Jun	Main Hall, Hatfield Polytechnic, Hatfield, England
26 Jun	Free Concert, Amsterdamse Bos, Amsterdam, The Netherlands
1 Jul	Musik-Forum Ossiachersee 1971, Congress Center, Villach, Austria (with orchestra and choir)
6 Aug	'71 Hakone Aphrodite, Fuji-Hakone-Izu National Park, Hakone, Japan
7 Aug	'71 Hakone Aphrodite, Fuji-Hakone-Izu National Park, Hakone, Japan
9 Aug	Festival Hall, Osaka, Japan
13 Aug	Festival Hall, Melbourne, Australia
15 Aug	St Leger Stand, Randwick Racecourse, Sydney, Australia
18 Sep	Festival de Musique Classique, Pavillion de Montreux, Montreux, Switzerland (with orchestra and choir)
19 Sep	Festival de Musique Classique, Pavillion de Montreux, Montreux, Switzerland (with orchestra and choir)
22 Sep	Kungliga Tennishallen, Stockholm, Sweden
23 Sep	KB Hallen, Copenhagen, Denmark
30 Sep	BBC Paris Cinema, Lower Regent Street, London, England

4 Oct Roman Ampitheater, Pompeii, Italy (Live in Pompeii recording)

5 Oct Roman Ampitheater, Pompeii, Italy (Live in Pompeii recording)

6 Oct Roman Ampitheater, Pompeii, Italy (Live in Pompeii recording)

7 Oct Roman Ampitheater, Pompeii, Italy (Live in Pompeii recording)

10 Oct Great Hall, Bradford University, Bradford, England

11 Oct Town Hall, Birmingham, England

15 Oct Winterland Auditorium, San Francisco, CA, USA

16 Oct Civic Auditorium, Santa Monica, CA, USA

17 Oct Convention Hall, Community Concourse, San Diego, CA, USA

19 Oct National Guard Armory, Eugene, OR, USA

21 Oct Salem Armory Auditorium, Salem, OR, USA

22 Oct Paramount Theater, Seattle, WA, USA

23 Oct Garden Auditorium, Vancouver, B.C., Canada

26 Oct Eastown Theater, Detroit, MI, USA

27 Oct Auditorium Theater, Chicago, IL, USA

28 Oct Hill Auditorium, University of Michigan, Ann Arbor, MI, USA

30 Oct Taft Auditorium, Cincinnati, OH, USA

31 Oct Fieldhouse, University of Toledo, Toledo, OH, USA

2 Nov McCarter Theatre, Princeton University, Princeton, NJ, USA

3 Nov Central Theatre, Passaic, NJ, USA

4 Nov Music Hall, Boston, MA, USA

4 Nov Loew's Theatre, Providence, RI, USA

5 Nov Loew's Theatre, Providence, RI, USA

5 Nov Assembly Hall, Hunter College, Columbia University of New York, New York City, NY, USA

6 Nov Emerson Gymnasium, Case Western Reserve University, Cleveland, OH, USA

8 Nov Peace Bridge Exhibition Center, Buffalo, NY, USA

9 Nov Centre Sportif, Université de Montréal, Montréal, Québec, Canada

10 Nov Pavillion de la Jeunesse, Québec City, Québec, Canada

11 Nov Music Hall, Boston, MA, USA

12 Nov Irvine Auditorium, University of Pennsylvania, Philadelphia, PA, USA

13 Nov Chapin Hall, Williams College, Williamstown, MA, USA

14 Nov Pritchard Gymnasium, State University of New York, Stony Brook, Long Island, NY, USA

15 Nov Main Hall, Carnegie Hall, New York City, NY, USA

16 Nov Lisner Auditorium, George Washington University, Washington D.C., USA

19 Nov Syria Mosque Theater, Pittsburgh, PA, USA

20 Nov Taft Auditorium, Cincinnati, OH, USA

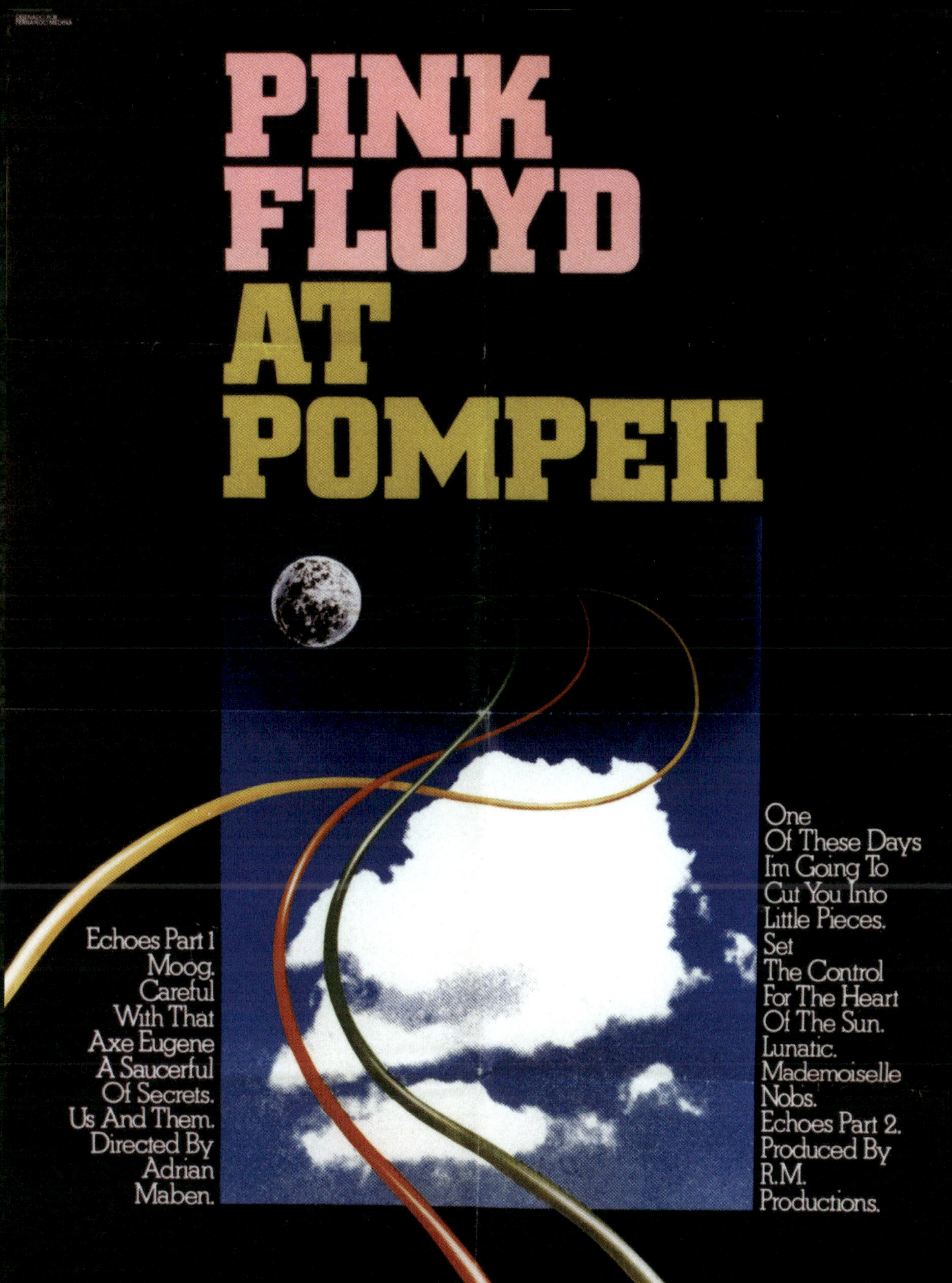
PINK FLOYD
AT POMPEII
Echoes Part 1
Moog.
Careful
With That
Axe Eugene
A Saucerful
Of Secrets.
Us And Them.
Directed By
Adrian
Maben.
One
Of These Days
I'm Going To
Cut You Into
Little Pieces.
Set
The Control
For The Heart
Of The Sun.
Lunatic.
Mademoiselle
Nobs.
Echoes Part 2.
Produced By
R.M.
Productions.

THE DARK SIDE OF THE MOON

'I had a very strong feeling when we finished the record that we had come up with something very, very special'

Roger Waters on album The Dark Side of the Moon

Between January 20 1972 and November 4 1973. Pink Floyd performed 118 concerts around the world, playing material from the Dark Side of the Moon album. The disc wasn't released until March 1973 but as was usual, they played the songs live several months beforehand when still a work in progress. Prior to embarking on a 16 date UK tour in January 1972, Floyd booked out the Rainbow Theatre in north London for three solid days of rehearsal. Their stage show would have a new look – and sound. Their first custom-built, state-of-the-art lighting rig was built to their specification by US lighting designer, Arthur Max; a new, PA system with a 28-channel mixing desk and four-channel 360-degree quadraphonic sound system was procured; and specially recorded backing tapes were created to be played on stage. Three giant trucks transported the nine tons of equipment.

The first gig of the year was at The Dome in Brighton with the plan being to road-test up to 40 minutes of new material.

'The Floyd opened the first set of the British tour with a new piece, tentatively "The Dark Side of the Moon" and showed that their writing had taken on a new and again innovatory form,' wrote the New Musical Express. *'A pulsating bass beat, pre-recorded, pounded around the hall's speaker system. A voice declared Chapter Five, versus 15 to 17 from the "Book of Ephesians". The organ built up, suddenly it soared like a jumbo jet leaving Heathrow; the lights just behind the equipment, rose like an elevator. Floyd were on stage, playing a medium-paced piece. The Floyd inventiveness had returned, and it astounded the capacity house.'*

Although not for the second half. A technical glitch during "Money" meant the band had to scale back the production.

'Due to severe mechanical and electric horror we can't do any more of that bit, so we'll do something else,' announced Roger Waters before briefly stalking off the stage.

However, the four shows at the Rainbow that closed the tour were hailed as a triumph.

On March 6, having chartered a DC 8 plane, Pink Floyd began a whistle-stop tour of Japan beginning in Tokyo and ending on 13 March in Sapporo.

'Their study of instruments is so impeccable and their techniques in handling them are marvellous,' reported Music Life.

A month later saw them take off to the US for a 17-date tour where at each gig, they played for three hours with only a short interval.

'It was a comparatively straight-forward tour,' Nick Mason remembers. *'It was part of a band's life that you had to try and build the audience base in the States. We were by now several years into the process and although we had not yet had a really successful album, we were able to fill the larger auditoria. Once formally engaged in the process of cracking America, it goes on forever.'*

From the US, Floyd travelled to West Germany for a handful of appearances, include one on the second day of the three-day '2nd British Rock Meeting' festival in Germersheim. Other bands on the bill included The Kinks, The Faces, and Status Quo. Once back home, they began a month-long recording session at Abbey Road studios, working out titles for the songs that would make up The Dark Side of The Moon album. Then in late June, they played the first of two shows at Brighton's Dome, as a replacement for the abandoned show in January.

September saw the band return to North America for a 17-date American and Canadian tour, opening at Austin, Texas' Municipal Auditorium and ending with a matinee and evening performance at Vancouver's Gardens Arena. The momentum was building. They booked into the iconic Hollywood Bowl which was far bigger than the 12,000-seater stadia they usually played. Although the show failed to sell out, it was a stunning showcase for their new material while the lightshow was the most

spectacular they had ever staged.

'We hired four of those searchlights that they use at film premieres,' said David Gilmour. *'We fanned them out backstage and pointed them at the sky, creating a pyramid on stage.'*

Returning to the UK in October, Floyd sold out Wembley Empire Pool for a charity benefit gig, filling the stage with dry ice, detonating flash bombs and setting alight the famous gong as they played 'Set the Controls for the Heart of the Sun'.

Sounds music newspaper couldn't praise the show highly enough.

'From the word go, they gave the packed stadium a faultless demonstration of what psychedelic music is all about. There wasn't a note, or a sound out of place during the whole evening. It's a recital more than a concert. All the time, the group were effectively illuminated by their imposing lighting tower at the rear of the stage which served a dual purpose – at frequent intervals it belched out smoke which mingled with the coloured lights and the dry ice surface mist to effectively whisk us all away to Planet Floyd.'

After more time in the studio working on 'The Dark Side of the Moon', throughout November Floyd snuck in several European dates before arriving in Paris in order to provide the music for a production by Les Ballets de Marseille.

'It did,' Nick Mason later said, *'appeal to certain intellectual quality among us.'*

Following this, their European tour continued in France, Belgium and Switzerland. As 1973 dawned, the Floyd returned to Paris for a second stint with the ballet. However, there would not be a third.

'The reality of all these people prancing around in tights in front of us didn't feel like what we wanted to do,' revealed Gilmour.

Pink Floyd perform live on stage at Amsterdam Rock Circus at the Olympisch Stadium on May 22 1972

Midway through January, the band returned to the studio to put the finishing touches to 'Dark Side of the Moon', with session singer Clare Torry recording her vocal for the song 'The Great Gig in The Sky'. The priority in 1973 was to finally crack the US and, for the first time, touring across the pond took priority to gigging in Europe. In March, 'Dark Side of the Moon' was released – firstly in the US and then the UK – and, as the album went to the top of the US charts, the band embarked on a 16-date US tour. They were joined by saxophonist Dick Parry – an old friend of Gilmour's – and backing vocalists Nawasa Crowder, and sisters Phyllis and Mary Ann Lindsey. Arthur Max's lighting creations had to be seen to be believed.

'Arthur was responsible for introducing the Genie Tower to our tours,' Nick Mason was to later say. *'These towers were one of the most important innovations in rock staging. Arthur had seen these hydraulic towers being used to change light bulbs in a factory and adapted the principle to allow them to carry racks of spotlights. For shows that had insufficient set-up time for rigging regular stage lighting or were out on a field on a stage made out of flat-bed trailers, these towers were a godsend. The fact that they could also be raised as an opening to the show was the icing on the cake. This was also the period when we brought in the circular screen backdrop.'*

According to Mason, one of Arthur's greatest shows for the band was at Radio City Music Hall in New York in March 1973. The stage contained six sections which could each raise 20 feet before moving forward. A 'steam curtain' was in front of the stage – a tube was drilled with holes that sent out a blast of steam to obscure the stage. This meant that an audience could enter the auditorium and see nothing but a bare stage. As the show began, the steam evaporated revealing the stage set, complete with the band's equipment, slowly rising while police lights attached to the Genie lighting towers flashed away. Floyd, with clouds of coloured smoke billowing around their ankles, began to play – the 20-speaker quad system blasting out the throbbing heartbeat and chiming clock of 'Dark Side of the Moon'.

'The Floyd were at their best,' reported Sounds, *'and the stage presentation was one of the best seen in a hell of a long time.'*

Their two shows at Earl's Court Exhibition Hall in London in May were just as impressive.

'Rockets were shooting out of the stage during "Money",' wrote the Record Mirror reviewer. *'"Breathe in the Air" followed with aeroplane sounds, spotlights scanning the roof, crashing into the stage and exploding.'*

In June, 'Pink Floyd' returned to the US for their second American tour of the year. They played 11 shows, starting at New York's Saratoga Performing Arts Centre and ending at Florida's Tampa Stadium. On the opening night at the Union City Roosevelt Stadium, they broke all box office records. Through Detroit, Ohio and Kentucky, the majority of dates were sold out. With the success of 'Dark Side of the Moon' and their astonishing stage shows, Floyd had finally broken America. But there was, they discovered, a downside.

'Everywhere we played, we suddenly found ourselves confronted with an audience that just wanted to hear the big hit,' said David Gilmour. *'"Play Money, play Money. . ." – that's all you'd hear throughout the show until we finally played it.'*

Floyd's last live date of 1973 was a two-show benefit performance at London's Rainbow Theatre in November '73 for 'Soft Machine' drummer Robert Wyatt who'd been paralysed from the waist down after falling from a four-storey window. It was the last live date they would play for 19 months. . .

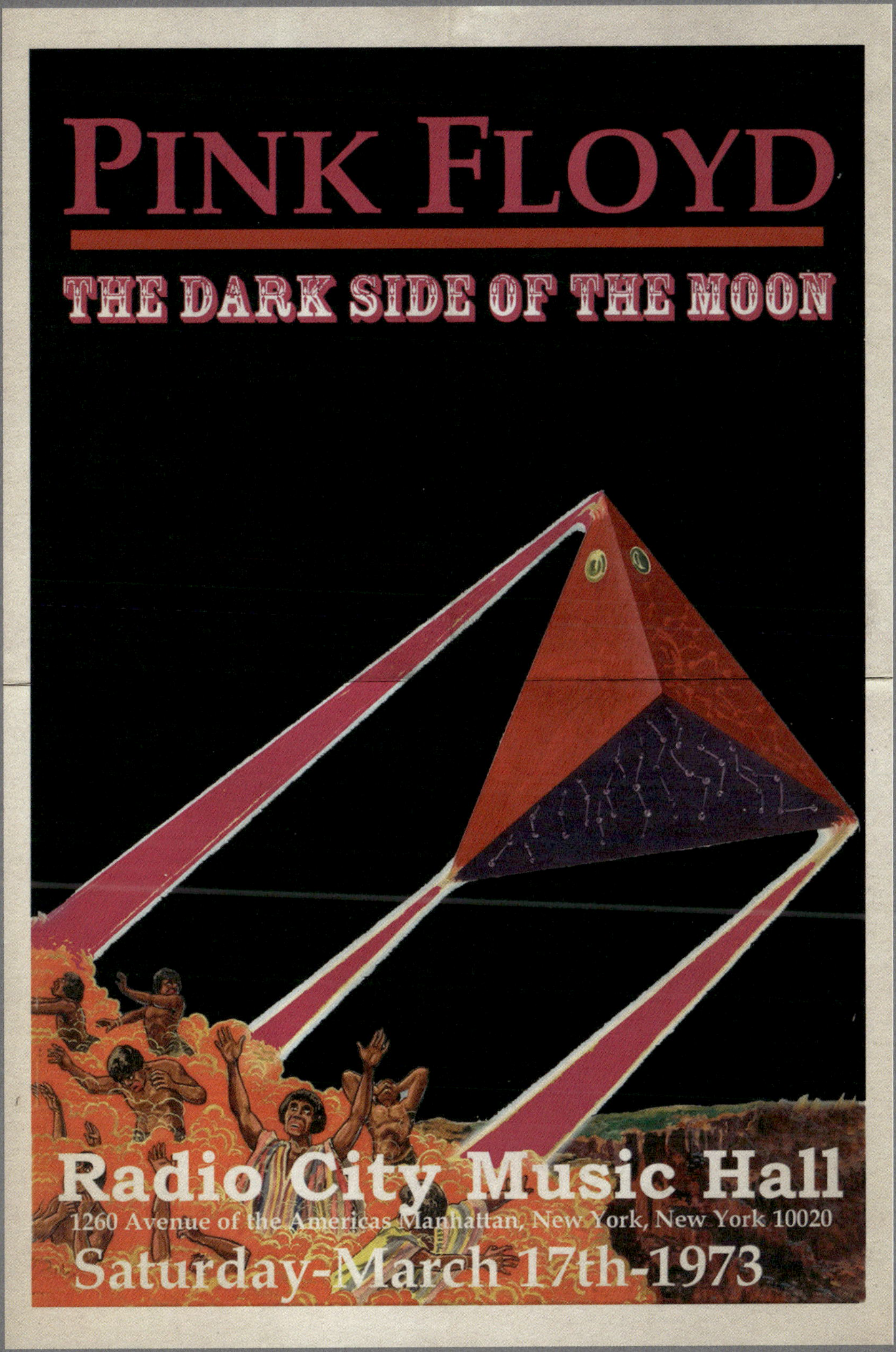
PINK FLOYD
THE DARK SIDE OF THE MOON
Radio City Music Hall
1260 Avenue of the Americas Manhattan, New York, New York 10020
Saturday-March 17th-1973

1972

'Sometimes I look at our huge trucks and tons of equipment and think, "Christ, I'm only playing an organ"'

Rick Wright

Typical set list:

- The Dark Side of the Moon
- One of Those Days
- Careful with that Axe, Eugene
- Echoes
- Set the Controls for the Heart of the Sun
- Obscured by the Clouds
- When You're In

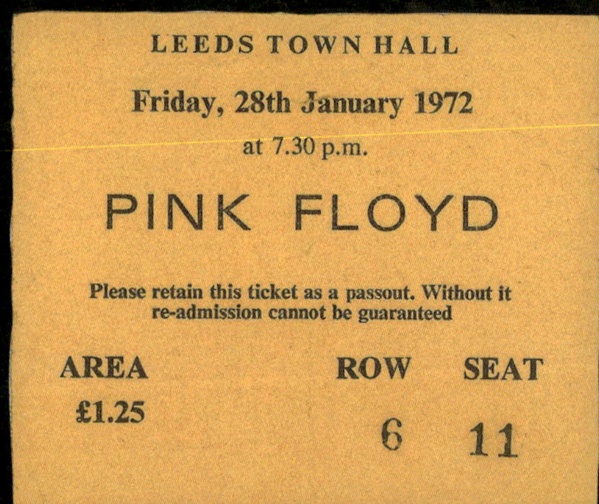

20 Jan The Dome, Brighton, England
21 Jan Guildhall, Portsmouth, England
22 Jan Winter Gardens, Bournemouth, England
23 Jan Guildhall, Southampton, England
27 Jan City Hall, Newcastle-Upon-Tyne, England
28 Jan Town Hall, Leeds, England
3 Feb Lanchester Polytechnic College Arts Festival, Locarno Ballroom, Coventry, England
5 Feb Colston Hall, Bristol, England
10 Feb De Montfort Hall, Leicester, England
12 Feb City (Oval) Hall, Sheffield, England
13 Feb The Empire Theatre, Liverpool, England
17 Feb Rainbow Theatre, Finsbury Park, London, England
18 Feb Rainbow Theatre, Finsbury Park, London, England
19 Feb Rainbow Theatre, Finsbury Park, London, England
20 Feb Rainbow Theatre, Finsbury Park, London, England
6 Mar Tokyo-To Taiikukan, Tokyo, Japan
7 Mar Tokyo-To Taiikukan, Tokyo, Japan
8 Mar Festival Hall, Osaka, Japan
9 Mar Festival Hall, Osaka, Japan
10 Mar Dai-Sho-Gun Furitsu Taiikukan, Kyoto, Japan
13 Mar Nakajima Sports Center, Sapporo, Japan
29 Mar Free Trade Hall, Manchester, England
30 Mar Free Trade Hall, Manchester, England
14 Apr Fort Homer Hesterly Armory Auditorium, Tampa, FL, USA
15 Apr The Sportatorium, Hollywood, FL, USA
16 Apr Township Auditorium, Columbia, SC, USA
18 Apr Symphony Hall, Atlanta Memorial Arts Center Atlanta, GA, USA
20 Apr The Syria Mosque Theater, Pittsburgh, PA, USA
21 Apr Lyric Theater, Baltimore, MD, USA
22 Apr Civic Theater, Akron, OH, USA
23 Apr Music Hall, Cincinnati, OH, USA
24 Apr Allen Theatre, Cleveland, OH, USA
26 Apr Ford Auditorium, Detroit, MI, USA
27 Apr Ford Auditorium, Detroit, MI, USA
28 Apr The Auditorium Theater, Chicago, IL, USA
29 Apr Spectrum Theater, Philadelphia, PA, USA
1 May Carnegie Hall, New York City, NY, USA
2 May Carnegie Hall, New York City, NY, USA
3 May Concert Hall, John F Kennedy Center for Performing Arts, Washington, Washington DC, USA
4 May Music Hall, Boston, MA, USA
18 May Deutschlandhalle, West Berlin, West Germany
21 May 2nd British Rock Meeting, Insel Grun, Germersheim, West Germany
22 May Amsterdam Rock Circus, Olympisch Stadium, Amsterdam, The Netherlands
28 Jun The Dome, Brighton, Sussex, England
29 Jun The Dome, Brighton, Sussex, England
8 Sep Municipal Auditorium, Austin, TX, USA

9 Sep Music Hall, Houston, TX, USA
10 Sep McFarlin Auditorium, Southern Methodist University, Dallas, TX, USA
11 Sep Memorial Hall, Kansas City, KS, USA
12 Sep Civic Center Music Hall, Oklahoma City, OK, USA
13 Sep Henry Levitt Arena, Wichita, KS, USA
15 Sep Community Center Arena, Tuscon, AZ, USA
16 Sep Golden Hall, Community Concourse, San Diego, CA, USA
17 Sep Big Surf, Tempe, AZ, USA
19 Sep University of Denver Arena, Denver, CO, USA
22 Sep Hollywood Bowl, Los Angeles, CA, USA
23 Sep Winterland Auditorium, San Francisco, CA, USA
24 Sep Winterland Auditorium, San Francisco, CA, USA

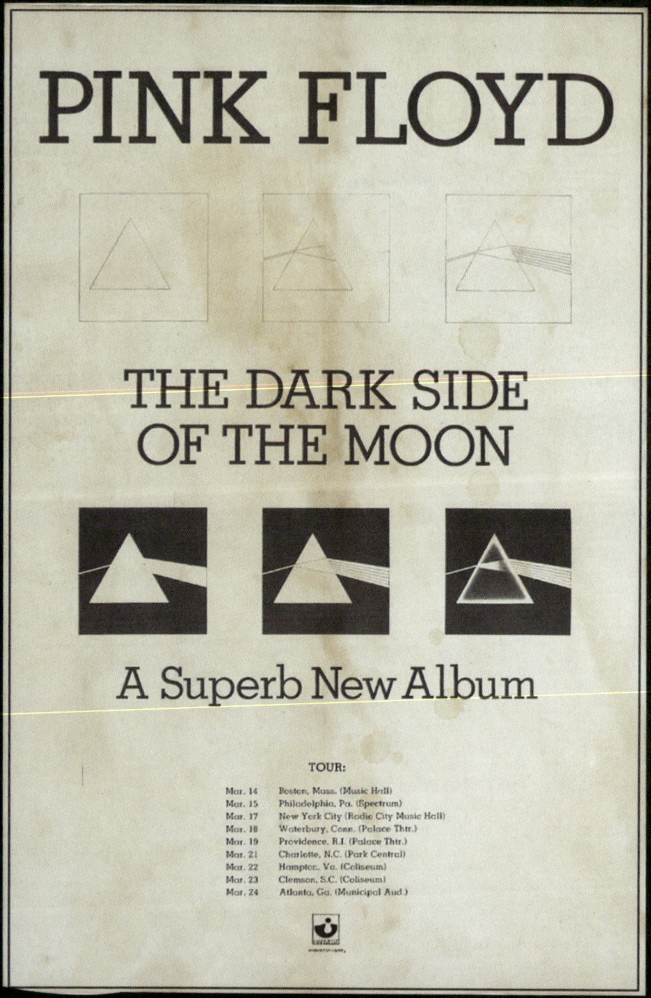

27 Sep Gardens Arena, Vancouver, BC, Canada
28 Sep Memorial Coliseum, Portland, OR, USA
29 Sep Hec Edmundson Pavilion, University of Washington, Seattle, WA, USA
30 Sep Vancouver Gardens Arena, Vancouver, BC, Canada)
21 Oct Empire Pool, Wembley, London, England
10 Nov KB Hallen, Copenhagen, Denmark
11 Nov KB Hallen, Copenhagen, Denmark
12 Nov Ernst Merck Halle, Hamburg, West Germany
14 Nov Philipshalle, Dusseldorf, West Germany
15 Nov Sporthalle, Boblingen, West Germany
16 Nov Festhalle, Frankfurt, West Germany
17 Nov Festhalle, Frankfurt, West Germany
22 Nov Roland Petit Ballet, Salle Valliers, Marseilles, France
23 Nov Roland Petit Ballet, Salle Valliers, Marseilles, France
24 Nov Roland Petit Ballet, Salle Valliers, Marseilles, France
25 Nov Roland Petit Ballet, Salle Valliers, Marseilles, France
26 Nov Roland Petit Ballet, Salle Valliers, Marseilles, France
28 Nov Palais des Sports, Toulouse, France
29 Nov Les Arènas, Parc des Expositions, Poitiers, France
1 Dec Centre Sportif, Ile des Vannes, Paris, France
2 Dec Centre Sportif, Ile des Vannes, Paris, France
3 Dec Parc des Expositions, Caen, France
5 Dec Sport Palais Vorst Nationaal, Brussels, Belgium
7 Dec Palais des Sports, Lille, France
8 Dec Parc des Expositions, Nancy, France
9 Dec Hallenstadion, Zurich, Switzerland
10 Dec Palais des Sports, Lyon, France

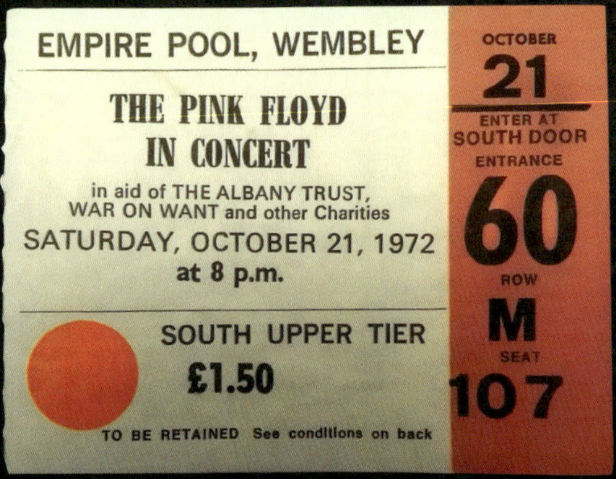

Good News & SUPER POP MONTREUX
present exclusively IN CONCERT:
PINK FLOYD
Samstag, 9. Dez. 72, 18.30 h
Hallenstadion Zürich
Tickets: Fr. 22.–
VORVERKAUF:
Zürich: Hallenstadion, Tel. (01) 46 30 30, Jelmoli, Jecklin, Hug
Wetzikon: Rewi-
Montreux: Office du Tourisme
Aarau: Coop-City
Luzern: Grammo-Studio
Winterthur: Pick Up
St. Gallen: Musik Hug
Basel: Boîte à Musique
Chur:
Schaffhausen: Music-Center Groner
Bern: Musik-Bestgen
Biel: Büchermarkt
Genève: Grand Passage SA
Neuchâtel: Hug & Cie.
Lausanne: Maurice & Pierre
Bitte Vorverkauf benützen!

1973

13 Jan Roland Petit Ballet, Paris, France
14 Jan Roland Petit Ballet, Paris, France
3 Feb Roland Petit Ballet, Paris, France
4 Feb Roland Petit Ballet, Paris, France
4 Mar Dane County Memorial Coliseum, Madison, WI, USA
5 Mar Cobo Arena, Detroit, MI, USA
6 Mar Kiel Auditorium, St. Louis, MS, USA
7 Mar International Amphitheater, Chicago, IL, USA
8 Mar Uni of Cincinnati Fieldhouse, Cincinnati, OH, USA
10 Mar Memorial Gymnasium, Kent State University, Kent, OH, USA
11 Mar Maple Leaf Gardens, Toronto, Ontario, Canada
12 Mar Forum de Montréal, Montréal, Québec, Canada
14 Mar Music Hall, Boston, MA, USA
15 Mar Spectrum Theater, Philadelphia, PA, USA
17 Mar Radio City Music Hall, New York City, NY, USA

18 Mar Palace Theater, Waterbury, CT, USA
19 Mar Providence Civic Center, Providence, RI, USA
22 Mar Hampton Coliseum, Hampton, VI, USA
23 Mar Charlotte Park Center, Charlotte, NC, USA
24 Mar Municipal Auditorium, Atlanta, GA, USA
18 May Earls Court Exhibition Hall, London, England
19 May Earls Court Exhibition Hall, London, England
17 Jun Performing Arts Center, Saratoga, NY, USA
18 Jun Roosevelt Stadium, Jersey City, NJ, USA
19 Jun Civic Center Arena, Pittsburgh, PA, USA
20 Jun Merriweather Post Pavilion, Columbia, MD, USA
21 Jun Merriweather Post Pavilion, Columbia, MD, USA
22 Jun Buffalo Memorial Auditorium, Buffalo, NY, USA
23 Jun Olympia Stadium, Detroit, MI, USA
24 Jun Blossom Music Center, Cuyahoga Falls, OH, USA
25 Jun Convention Center, Louisville, KY, USA
27 Jun Jacksonville Coliseum, Jacksonville, FL, USA
28 Jun The Sportatorium, Hollywood, FL, USA
29 Jun Tampa Stadium, Tampa, FL, USA
12 Oct Munchener Olympiahalle, Olympia Park, Munich, West Germany
13 Oct Stadthalle, Vienna, Austria
4 Nov A Benefit For Robert Wyatt, Rainbow Theatre, London, England

The Pink Floyd

15p

SUPER ALL-ACTION *OFFICIAL* MUSIC PROGRAMME FOR BOYS AND GIRLS!

WISH YOU WERE HERE?

'We were all rather badly mentally ill – we were completely exhausted for one reason or another'

Roger Waters after the phenomenon that was 'Dark Side of the Moon'

In early 1974, Floyd's first two albums 'The Piper at the Gates of Dawn' and 'A Saucerful of Secrets' were re-issued as a double album package, titled 'A Nice Pair'. But it wasn't until June of that year that they went back out on the road, by which time, two new songs, 'Raving and Drooling' and 'Shine On' (later changed to 'Shine on You Crazy Diamond) had been written. The tour comprised of exclusively French dates but problems began to surface before they had even played their first gig. The stage set had been re-designed to create visuals even more spectacular than the previous year. A 40-foot circular screen – known as 'Mr Screen' by the band – was now to be positioned at the back of the stage, upon which would be projected specially filmed 35 mm footage and animation sequences, designed by Birmingham art student, Ian Eames. During 'Shine On', footage of a massive rotating mirror ball would be projected onto the screen, coupled with the beam of a spotlight thus producing lazer-like beams of white light. Fireworks and rockets were also part of this dazzling light show. However, when the tour's promoters realised just how much voltage was required to power this extravaganza in addition to how high the venues' ceilings needed to be to accommodate the giant screen, several gigs were cancelled. To complicate issues further, throughout the tour, Floyd were shadowed by Parisienne 'trend-setters' as part

Pink Floyd on stage in France, 1974

of a sponsorship deal with a soft drink's company.

'Our hard-earner credibility with our French fans was left in tatters,' recalls Nick Mason.

It wasn't until November '74 that Floyd embarked on a 20-date tour of the UK. The 'British Winter Tour' began at Edinburgh's Usher Hall and ended at Bristol's Hippodrome. New film sequences of sweeping urban landscapes, slowed-down rush-hour footage, hysterical politicians, South African diamond miners, flying clock faces, and underwater shots – to name but a few – had been filmed to project on the circular screen, and before setting out on tour, the band had three intense weeks of rehearsals in a film studio in order to be 'in sync' with the visuals. The tour included four nights at London's Wembley Empire Pool, London, one of which was broadcast on BBC Radio One. The amended set list included a third new composition, 'You've Got to be Crazy'. The tour programme, titled 'The Pink Floyd Super All-Action Official Music Programme for Boys and Girls', was printed as a comic and featured a band portrait by eminent cartoonist Gerald Scarfe and cartoon strips of the band members depicted as their alter egos 'Rog of The Rovers', 'Captain Mason R.N.', 'Rich Right' and 'Dave Derring'. All the shows sold out, however, behind the scenes there were problems with equipment and crew personnel plus it appeared that the music press were beginning to turn on them.

'Floyd always let their songs sprawl out to last twice as long as they should,' remarked New Musical Express while The Bristol Evening Post reported that the gig at the Hippodrome in the city was *'an irritating, disappointing show which never even looked like taking off'.*

Nick Mason was to later admit that it hadn't been the best of times for Floyd.

'It was a gloomy time for us – although hopefully audiences weren't aware of this. As a band we were demonstrating a distinct lack of commitment and the necessary input required. As a result, our shows were a wildly erratic mix of the good and bad and occasionally ugly – both technically and musically. After the way the Earls Court performances in 1973 had gelled so perfectly, the problems we experienced on this tour added to our frustration, and to the sense that we were all pulling in slightly different directions. I think it might be true to say we were close to calling it a day. Eventually we managed to pull ourselves into some semblance of order but we were all grateful when Christmas arrived and the tour ended.'

'Pink Floyd did a live show that depends on gadgets and an excellent 360-degree sound system'

The Vancouver Sun's review after their show in the Canadian city in April 1975

1974

'Pink Floyd spent most of 1974 delaying the evil moment of making a record'

Nick Mason

Typical set list:

Shine on You Crazy Diamond Raving and Drooling (later Sheep) You've Got to Be Crazy (later Dogs) Speak to Me Breathe On the Run Time The Great Gig in the Sky Money Us and Them Any Colour You Like Brain Damage Eclipse Echoes

18 Jun	Hall 1, Parc des Expositions, Toulouse, France	5 Nov	Usher Hall, Edinburgh, Scotland
19 Jun	Les Arènas, Parc des Expositions, Poitiers, France	8 Nov	Odeon, Newcastle-upon-Tyne, England
21 Jun	Hall 1, Palais des Expositions, Dijon, France	9 Nov	Odeon, Newcastle-upon-Tyne, England
22 Jun	Théâtre de Plein Air, Parc des Expositions, Colmar, France	14 Nov	Empire Pool, Wembley, London, England
24 Jun	Palais des Sports de la Porte de Versailles, Paris, France	15 Nov	Empire Pool, Wembley, London, England
25 Jun	Palais des Sports de la Porte de Versailles, Paris, France	16 Nov	Empire Pool, Wembley, London, England
26 Jun	Palais des Sports de la Porte de Versailles, Paris, France	17 Nov	Empire Pool, Wembley, London, England
4 Nov	Usher Hall, Edinburgh, Scotland	19 Nov	Trentham Gardens, Stoke-on-Trent, England

Parc des Expositions - TOULOUSE
CONCERT
PINK FLOYD
MARDI 18 JUIN 1974, 21 heures
25 f
Nº 00630
Droit de location perçu en sus : 1 F.
Timbre réglé sur état en accord avec le Trésor.
Imp. Duchaussoy, Aulnay-sous-Bois

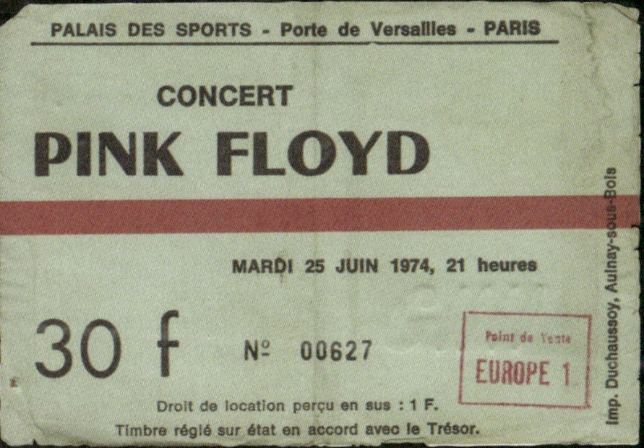
PALAIS DES SPORTS - Porte de Versailles - PARIS
CONCERT
PINK FLOYD
MARDI 25 JUIN 1974, 21 heures
30 f
Nº 00627
Point de Vente
EUROPE 1
Droit de location perçu en sus : 1 F.
Timbre réglé sur état en accord avec le Trésor.
Imp. Duchaussoy, Aulnay-sous-Bois

USHER HALL
EDINBURGH
Doors open 7.00 pm
Tuesday
5 November 1974
at 7.30 pm
Harvey Goldsmith for John Smith Entertainments
presents
PINK FLOYD
IN CONCERT
C 21
UPPER
TIER
£1.80
Inc. V.A.T
RESERVED
ENTER BY SIDE DOOR GRINDLAY STREET
NO TICKET EXCHANGED OR MONEY REFUNDED
RETAIN THIS PORTION

GINI...
Bitter lemon tonic
présente
PINK FLOYD
7 concerts en France
en première mondiale avec
EUROPE 1
TOULOUSE ...... le 18 Juin 74 (Parc des Expositions)
POITIERS ...... le 19 Juin 74 (Parc des Expositions)
LYON ...... le 21 Juin 74 (Palais des Sports)
COLMAR ...... le 22 Juin 74 (Parc des Expositions)
PARIS ...... les 24-25-26 Juin 74 (Palais des Sports)

From early January 1975, Pink Floyd began an intermittent three months of recording at Abbey Road studios for their next album, 'Wish You Were Here'. Relations between the band members continued to be fraught.

'At the "Wish You Were Here" recording sessions, most of us didn't wish we were there at all,' Roger Waters was later to say. *'We wished we were somewhere else.'*

The sessions were interrupted by the first leg of Floyd's North American Tour – 14 dates which kicked off on April 8 at Vancouver's Pacific National Exhibition Coliseum. As with the previous year's shows, the band were joined on stage by additional personnel – saxophonist Dick Parry, and backing singers Carlena Williams and Venetta Fields. Within hours of the tour being announced just a month before it started, several shows sold out breaking box office records. In just a single day, the four shows at the Los Angeles Sports Arena completely sold out – and a hastily arranged fifth show followed suit.

The band's special effects now included a model aircraft which flew over the audience and crashed during the Dark Side of the Moon section, in addition to a veritable arsenal of pyrotechnics which were more professional, sophisticated and – most importantly – safe than their previous explosive exploits on stage. In a fortuitous move, Floyd were lucky enough to employ the services of special effects experts who had worked on the James Bond movies. In addition to the explosions, 'Mr Screen' displayed cartoonist Gerald Scarfe's quirky imagery. The fans lapped it up but once again some critics weren't impressed.

'A light show is a good addition to most rock shows,' reported a student newspaper in Arizona, *'but when special effects are carried to the extreme, they can only detract from the music and create a carnival atmosphere. The music was good enough to outweigh the gimmicks, however. And let it said that their 32 tons of equipment was enough. My ears were ringing for hours after the show.'*

The tour was also tainted by allegations of ticket fraud, plus the tactics of the LAPD raised eyebrows when they arrested over 500 mostly peaceful fans over the five nights of shows, the majority for possession of marijuana.

Another mammoth recording session awaited Pink Floyd on their return to the UK in early May but a month later, they were back in North America for the second leg of their tour. The sports stadia in which they were due to play were such a size that their stage set seemed almost dwarfed.

'We were trying to incorporate more and more special effects,' Nick Mason recalls. *'Of these, the inflatable*

pyramid was perhaps our most spectacular disaster.'

This inflatable pyramid was the brain child of that former architecture student, Roger Waters – the aim of it being to float above the stage, anchored by cables, and mirror the prism on the cover of the 'Dark Side of the Moon' album. Problem was that when the 60 feet structure was inflated and powered with helium, the pyramid became impossible to control. It failed to inflate properly at the first gig in Atlanta but the date at the Three Rivers Stadium in Pittsburgh had a very different outcome. At the climax of the show, the inflated pyramid rose high into the air but due to strong winds it blew over, dislodging the balloon inside.

'The balloon emerged like a teardrop through the base,' Nick Mason recalled. *'One chemically-affected American shouted as it emerged: "My God, it's giving birth!" The fabric had insufficient lift so as the teardrop headed for the stratosphere, the world's biggest wet blanket settled ungracefully into the car park to be ripped to shreds by scavenging souvenir hunters.'*

On the final night of the tour in Ontario, Canada, the crew decided a fitting finale – once the band were off stage and the stadium cleared – would be to end things with *'the biggest, loudest, f**k off explosion ever'* and so one member attached the remaining explosives to the stadium's illuminated scoreboard.

'The explosion was devastating,' according to Nick Mason, *'with the scoreboard erupting in smoke and flames.'*

'Devastating' didn't come close. Half the stadium's back wall was blown out and also the windows from many surrounding houses.

Floyd lost no time in hot-footing back to the UK where on July 5, they played in the extensive grounds of Knebworth Park Stately Home. In such a setting and being supported by the likes of 'The Steve Miller Band', 'Captain Beefheart and his Magic Band' and Floyd's old friend Roy Harper, who would join them on stage to sing 'Have a Cigar', it should have been one of the most memorable shows in their almost 10-year-history. But. . .it wasn't. The crew were jet-lagged, arriving late to set up the band's equipment, where they made the discovery that the voltage of backstage generators kept fluctuating. As a result, Rick Wright's keyboards kept going out of tune and at one point during Floyd's set, the PA failed completely.

'Wish You Here' was released in the UK on September 12 1975 and in the US, a day later. The album went to the top of the charts in both countries but no tours were scheduled for the rest of the year. In fact, they wouldn't play another live date until January 1977.

1975

‘Personally, I’m not very keen on the visualization of absolutely everything’

David Gilmour

Typical set list:

SheepDogsShine on You Crazy DiamondHave a Cigar BreatheOn the RunTimeBreathe (reprise)The Great Gig in the SkyMoneyUs and ThemAny Colour You LikeBrain DamageEclipseEchoes

Apr Pacific National Exhibition Coliseum, Vancouver, B.C., Canada
0 Apr Seattle Center Coliseum, Seattle, WA, USA
2 Apr The Cow Palace, Daly City, San Francisco, CA, USA
3 Apr The Cow Palace, Daly City, San Francisco, CA, USA
7 Apr Denver Coliseum, Denver, CO, USA
9 Apr Tucson Community Center Arena, Tuscon, AZ, USA
0 Apr University Activity Center, Arizona State University, Tempe, AZ, USA
1 Apr Sports Arena, San Diego, CA, USA
2 Apr Los Angeles Memorial Sports Arena, Los Angeles, CA, USA
3 Apr Los Angeles Memorial Sports Arena, Los Angeles, CA, USA
4 Apr Los Angeles Memorial Sports Arena, Los Angeles, CA, USA
5 Apr Los Angeles Memorial Sports Arena, Los Angeles, CA, USA
6 Apr Los Angeles Memorial Sports Arena, Los Angeles, CA, USA
Jun Atlanta Stadium, Atlanta, GA, USA
Jun Capital Centre, Landover, MD, USA
10 Jun Capital Centre, Landover, MD, USA
12 Jun Spectrum Theater, Philadelphia, PA, USA
13 Jun Spectrum Theater, Philadelphia, PA, USA
15 Jun Roosevelt Stadium, Jersey City, NJ, USA
16 Jun Nassau Veterans Memorial Coliseum, Uniondale, Long Island, NY, USA
17 Jun Nassau Veterans Memorial Coliseum, Uniondale, Long Island, NY, USA
18 Jun Boston Gardens, Boston, MA, USA
20 Jun Three Rivers Stadium, Pittsburgh, PA, USA
22 Jun County Stadium, Milwaukee, WI, USA
23 Jun Olympia Stadium, Detroit, MI, USA
24 Jun Olympia Stadium, Detroit, MI, USA
26 Jun Autostade, Montréal, Québec, Canada
28 Jun Ivor Wynne Stadium, Hamilton, Ontario, Canada
5 Jul Knebworth Park, Stevenage, England

ANIMALS

'This was the start of the whole ego thing in the band'

Rick Wright

Following the release of the 'Wish You Were Here' album, Floyd spent 1976 firstly kitting out 'Brit Row', their new studio constructed from a three-storey block of former church halls in north London, before commencing eight months of continuous recording for their next album, which would be called 'Animals'. It was influenced by George Orwell's book '1984' with the hierarchy of animals being represented by Sheep (people), Dogs (police) and Pigs (masters and politicians). The album was very much Roger Waters 'baby' in which he pursued his own vision – ie, the animalistic behaviour of human beings. To such an extent that it began to isolate other members of the band.

'Roger was in full flow with the ideas but he was really keeping Dave down and frustrating him deliberately,' said Nick Mason.

Rick Wright felt similarly pushed out.

'I didn't contribute to the writing of it but I think also Roger was kind of not letting me do that,' he was later to say.

'Animals' was released on January 21 1977 in the UK and in the US on the 22nd. It reached Number Two in the former and Number Three in the latter – marginally lower than Floyd's two previous albums.

'I never expected "Animals" to sell as many as "Wish You Were Here" and 'Dark Side of the Moon",' David Gilmour commented. *'There's not a lot of sweet, sing-a-long stuff on it.'*

On the contrary. 'Animals' was the closest Pink Floyd had come to a heavy rock opus. It was described by the New Musical Express as *'bleak, dark and foreboding in mood, and another apparent progression in Waters' paranoia'.*

The European leg of 'Animals' tour began in January 1977 and changes had been made to the stage show. The sassy female backing singers of previous tours had been 'let go' but a second guitarist, heavy rocker Trevor 'Snowy' White, was recruited to join them on stage. The special effects were, as was to be expected, innovatively spectacular, including, for the first time, a pyrotechnic waterfall and umbrella-like canopies which would rise from the stage to protect the band from the elements. Then there were the giant inflatable puppets, secured by cables, that loomed over the stadia and venues as the band played. These comprised of a businessman, his wife and their 2.5 children sat on an inflatable sofa, and a pig – similar to the one on the album cover. Another element was a 'sheep cannon' that fired small sheep figures made from tea-bag fabric into the audience. Although visually mesmerising, in true Floyd tradition the special effects would prove problematic. . . The first three West German concerts of the tour started well enough but then it got messy – in more ways than one!

'It had been an evening totally without mishaps,' the review in 'Melody Maker' began. *'The 12,000 natives packed into Frankfurt's Festhalle for the second successive night were in a generally friendly mood for The Floyd hardly attract the same aggro crowd of people like Zep or Purple. But in an audience that size, it is a statistical certainty there are bound to be some nutters, like those who were throwing cans and bottles during the first set. An announcement in the interval asked them to desist, "bitte", because delicate equipment was getting damaged. I saw another bottle smash on Nick Mason's Hokusai painted*

Dave Gilmour, Circa 1977

drum kit – evidently a full one for it sprayed his face with foam.
n the shadow of the PA columns, a group of plain clothes "polizei", about as inconspicuous as a panzer armoured division n their uniform, anoraks and regulation-length haircuts, took photographs of the crowd to see if anyone was smoking dope. . The band's special effects department still hadn't got the highpoint of their contribution to the show quite right yet. In the middle of the "Pigs" section. . .a giant, inflated porker is meant to fly over the PA, emerging out of a cloud of smoke, clearing the stacks by a few inches, and making a circuit of the hall over the heads of the audience. Well, Mr Pig made it over the stack all right without toppling the driver horns on the top but the trouble was the smoke. The first three nights they couldn't get enough product out of the rented fog-machine, so they tried a smoke bomb instead. That worked rather too well for comfort, filling the hall with billowing clouds of acrid, throat-strangling murk, through which it was barely possible to see that something was happening on stage.'

The American leg of 'Animals', renamed as 'Pink Floyd in The Flesh', began in April with a and TV, refrigerator and Cadillac added to the 'family' of giant inflatables. As in Europe, there were technical problems with props and special effects. At the first show in Miami, high winds prevented 'Mr Screen' from being lowered into place while 'Mr Pig' was blown apart by strong gusts while inflating. At a later outdoor stadium show in Cleveland, Ohio, a newly-produced, fully blown-up porcine was hit by a firework launched by a punter in the audience, puncturing it and bringing it down into the crowd. It was also becoming clear that Roger Waters was barely holding it together. He deliberately isolated himself from the rest of the band, arriving at venues alone and shunning any post-gig festivities. The fact that he wore headphones on stage meant that there was little interaction with his bandmates. He was also exhibiting increasingly aggressive behaviour towards the fans, clearly bothered that the enormous audiences on this tour seemed more interested in partying rather than watching the show and contemplating the music and lyrics. He would often scold audiences, yelling and screaming at crowds who ignited fireworks, particularly during the quieter numbers.

*'You stupid mother**ker,'* he yelled into the crowd at one of the New York gigs. *'And anyone else here with fireworks – just f**k off and let us get on with it.'*

Matters came to a deeply unpleasant head at the final concert of the tour at the Olympic Stadium in Montreal, Canada on July 6. The audience was massive, rowdy, and many were drunk and/or stoned. Waters was already emotionally and mentally worn down from the tour and this was the day that he finally snapped.

'I was on stage and there was one guy in the front row, shouting and screaming all the way through everything,' Waters later recounted. *'In the end I called him over and, when he got close enough, I spat in his face. I shocked myself enough with that incident to think, "Hold on a minute. This is all wrong. I'm hating this".'*

Although the other members of Floyd seem not to have been aware of the incident, David Gilmour did not join the band on stage for the encore.

'I just thought it was a great shame to end up a six-month tour with a rotten show,' he recalled. *'In fact, I remember going back to the sound mixing board in the middle of the audience to watch the show while Snowy played guitar.'*

A small riot at the front of the stage followed the band's eventual exit.

'It was a funny gig,' recalled Snowy White. *'I just used to do my job but there was a really weird vibe and I looked across to see Roger spitting at this guy at the front. It was very strange.'*
It was also hanging in the balance whether the Floyd would ever play live again.

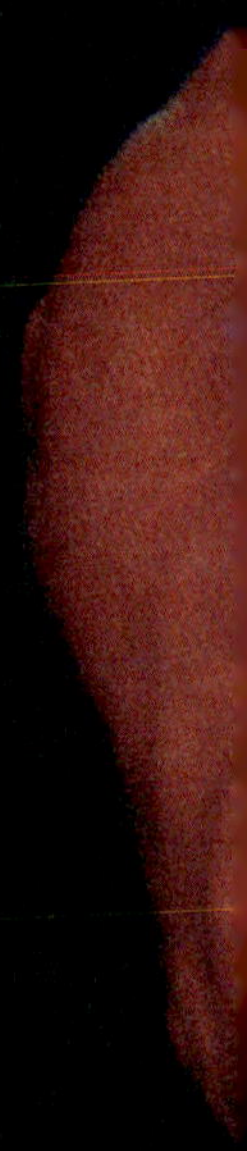

Roger Waters of Pink Floyd in concert at Anaheim Stadium on May 6, 1977 in Anaheim, California

1977

Typical set list:

Sheep
Pigs on the Wing, Part One
Pigs on the Wing, Part Two
Pigs, Three Different Ones
Shine On You Crazy Diamond, Parts One to Five
Welcome to the Machine
Have a Cigar
Wish You Were Here
Shine On You Crazy Diamond, Parts Six to Nine
Money
Us and Them

'It gets easier and easier to review a Pink Floyd concert without mentioning the music'

the The Financial newspaper, March 1977

23 Jan	Westfalenhalle, Dortmund, West Germany
24 Jan	Westfalenhalle, Dortmund, West Germany
26 Jan	Festhalle, Frankfurt, West Germany
27 Jan	Festhalle, Frankfurt, West Germany
29 Jan	Deutschlandhalle, West Berlin, West Germany
30 Jan	Deutschlandhalle, West Berlin, West Germany
1 Feb	Stadthalle, Vienna, Austria
3 Feb	Hallenstadion, Zurich, Switzerland
4 Feb	Hallenstadion, Zurich, Switzerland
17 Feb	Sportpaleis Ahoy, Rotterdam, The Netherlands
18 Feb	Sportpaleis Ahoy, Rotterdam, The Netherlands
19 Feb	Sportpaleis Ahoy, Rotterdam, The Netherlands
20 Feb	Sportpaleis, Antwerp, Belgium
22 Feb	Pavillion de Paris, Porte de Pantin, Paris, France
23 Feb	Pavillion de Paris, Porte de Pantin, Paris, France
24 Feb	Pavillion de Paris, Porte de Pantin, Paris, France
25 Feb	Pavillion de Paris, Porte de Pantin, Paris, France
27 Feb	Olympiahalle, Munich, West Germany
28 Feb	Olympiahalle, Munich, West Germany
1 Mar	Olympiahalle, Munich, West Germany
15 Mar	Empire Pool, Wembley, London, England
16 Mar	Empire Pool, Wembley, London, England
17 Mar	Empire Pool, Wembley, London, England
18 Mar	Empire Pool, Wembley, London, England
19 Mar	Empire Pool, Wembley, London, England
28 Mar	New Bingley Hall, Staffordshire County Showground, Stafford, England
29 Mar	New Bingley Hall, Staffordshire County Showground, Stafford, England
30 Mar	New Bingley Hall, Staffordshire County Showground, Stafford, England
31 Mar	New Bingley Hall, Staffordshire County Showground, Stafford, England
22 Apr	Miami Baseball Stadium, Miami, FL, USA
24 Apr	Tampa Stadium, Tampa, FL, USA
26 Apr	The Omni Coliseum, Atlanta, GA
28 Apr	Assembly Center, Louisiana State University, Baton Rouge, LA, USA
30 Apr	Jeppesen Stadium, University Of Houston, Houston, TX, USA
1 May	Tarrant County Convention Center, Forth Worth, TX, USA
4 May	Veterans Memorial Coliseum, Phoenix, AZ, USA
6 May	Anaheim Stadium, Anaheim, Los Angeles, CA, USA
7 May	Anaheim Stadium, Anaheim, Los Angeles, CA, USA
9 May	Oakland Coliseum Arena, Oakland, CA, USA
10 May	Oakland Coliseum Arena, Oakland, CA, USA
12 May	Memorial Coliseum, Portland, OR, USA
15 Jun	County Stadium, Milwaukee, WI, USA
17 Jun	Freedom Hall, Louisville, KY, USA
19 Jun	Super Bowl of Rock 'n' Roll, Soldier Field, Chicago, IL, USA
21 Jun	Kemper Arena, Kansas City, MO, USA
23 Jun	Riverfront Coliseum, Cincinnati, OH, USA
25 Jun	World Series of Rock, Municipal Stadium, Cleveland, OH, USA
27 Jun	Boston Garden, Boston, MA, USA
28 Jun	Spectrum Theater, Philadelphia, PA, USA
29 Jun	Spectrum Theater, Philadelphia, PA, USA
1 Jul	Madison Square Garden, New York City, NY, USA
2 Jul	Madison Square Garden, New York City, NY, USA
3 Jul	Madison Square Garden, New York City, NY, USA
4 Jul	Madison Square Garden, New York City, NY, USA
6 Jul	Stade du Parc Olympique, Montréal, Québec, Canada

PINK FLOYD
En chair et en os
PINK FLOYD
In the flesh
LE MERCREDI
6 JUILLET
20 H.
BEAU TEMPS, MAUVAIS TEMPS
Billets $10.00 en vente
chez tous les comptoirs T.R.S.
et aux guichets du Forum.
BOUTEILLES ET CANNETTES
NE SERONT PAS PERMISES A
L'INTERIEUR DU STADE OLYMPIQUE
WEDNESDAY
JULY 6 - 8 P.M.
RAIN OR SHINE
Tickets $10.00 on sale
at all T.R.S. outlets and
the Forum Box Office.
NO BOTTLES OR CANS PERMITTED
INTO THE OLYMPIC STADIUM
LE STADE OLYMPIQUE

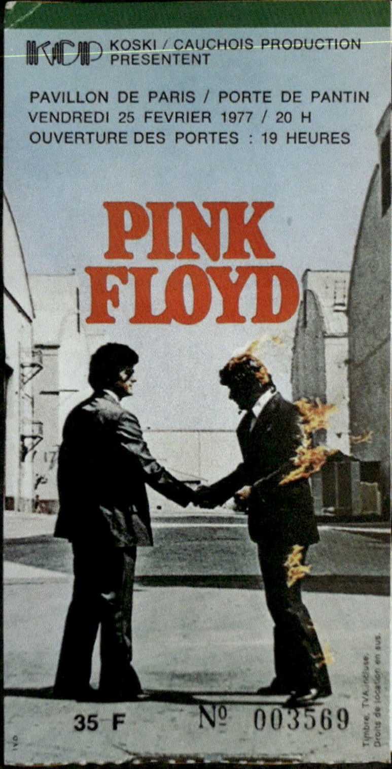
KOSKI / CAUCHOIS PRODUCTION
PRESENTENT
PAVILLON DE PARIS / PORTE DE PANTIN
VENDREDI 25 FEVRIER 1977 / 20 H
OUVERTURE DES PORTES : 19 HEURES
PINK
FLOYD
35 F
Nº 003569

PINK FLOYD
IN THE FLESH
HOUSTON'S JEPPESEN STADIUM
SATURDAY, APRIL 30th 8.00 p.m.
GENERAL ADMISSION $10.00
HOUSTON TICKETS AVAILABLE AT:
IN HOUSTON: WAREHOUSE RECORDS AND TAPES
MUSICVILLE
IN AUSTIN: RAYMOND'S DRUGS
IN SAN ANTONIO: JAM & JELLY GENERAL STORE
IN DALLAS: RAINBOW TICKETS
IN CORPUS CHRISTI: KALEIDOSCOPE
IN FT. WORTH: L. P. GOODBUY

BILL GRAHAM PRESENTS
PINK FLOYD
OAKLAND COLISEUM
MAY 9 & 10, 1977

THE WALL

'I was struck by the thought that there was a huge wall, that you couldn't see, between me and the audience. Then I drew it and started to talk to people about it. And they thought I was mad, because my original idea was to start building a wall at the beginning of the show and, when it's finished, they can't see you or hear you anymore, and then the show is over'

Roger Waters

Rogers Waters may have said he was ashamed by 'Spitgate' at the end of the 'In the Flesh' tour in 1977 but it gave him the impetus and idea for the next 'Pink Floyd' concept.

'I loathed playing in stadiums,' he later revealed. *'I kept saying to people on that tour, "I'm not really enjoying this. There's something very wrong with this". At a certain point, something in my brain snapped, and I developed the idea of doing a concert where we built a wall across the front of the stage that divided the audience from the performers.'*

The reaction of Mason, Gilmour and Wright to the idea was mixed.

'Roger's demo was like a skeleton with lots of bones missing,' Mason was later to say, *'but... what an idea.'*

Gilmour was less impressed.

'It was too depressing and boring in places,' he said, *'but I liked the basic idea.'*

Roger Waters performing live onstage — The Wall Concert, Earls Court, 1981

As for Wright? His relationship with Waters was breaking down to such an extent that it appeared to make little impact.

'The Wall' story was divided into two parts which would ultimately emerge as a double album. It's chief character, known as Pink, was, in effect, looking back on his life. The first half was very much influenced by Roger Waters' own life – the death of his father in World War Two when he'd been little more than a baby, his relationship with his over-protective mother and how he'd been bullied by school teachers during his education. The second half concentrated on Waters' view of the music business and what had happened to Syd Barrett.

Recording took place during 1978 and 79, and it was during this time that Rick Wright's relationship with Mason and Gilmour also began to deteriorate.

'Rick's relationship with all of us – and most certainly Roger – did become impossible during the making of "The Wall",' David Gilmour was later to say. *'He had been asked if he had any ideas or anything that he wanted to do. We would leave the studio in the evening and he would have the whole night to*

come up with stuff but he didn't contribute anything. He just sat there and it was driving us all mad.'

Finally, Waters announced he was giving Wright an ultimatum – said to be that either Rick come out early to Los Angeles in order to catch up on the backlog of work or leave the band. Wright was going through a messy divorce at the time and had seen very little of his children. After consideration, Wright decided to go – yet said he was still willing to perform at the live shows.

'It's quite simple,' he later explained. *'It started because Roger and I didn't get on. There was a lot of antagonism during "The Wall" and he said either you leave or I'll scrap everything we've done and there won't be an album. Normally I would have told him to get lost but at that point we had to earn money to pay off the back taxes we owed. Anyway, Roger said that if I didn't leave, he would re-record the material. I couldn't afford to say no so I left.'*

'The Wall' was released at the end of November 1979 in the UK and early December in the US. It reached Number Three in Britain and Number One in the States. In February 1980, Floyd went back on the road with the spectacular stage show that was 'The Wall'. It wasn't a tour in the traditional sense. Pink Floyd performed the album 31 times over the course of 16 months in only four cities – Los Angeles, New York, London (on two separate occasions) and and Dortmund, West Germany. Its scale and grandiosity were built into the concept from the very start by Roger Waters who, it has to be said, was becoming rather grand himself.

'We pretended that we are jolly good chaps together but that wasn't true,' he later claimed in an interview. *'I made the decisions. We pretended it was a democracy for a long time but this album was the big own-up. I always knew it would be a multi-faceted project — a record, followed by shows in just a few cities and then a movie. It couldn't possibly travel because of the sheer expense of getting this thing to move. It was miles ahead of anything that had been done in rock 'n 'roll and the amount of effort that went into every single detail was unheard of. It was very f**king difficult to do but we had some very good people on board who made it happen.'*

One of these *'very good people'* was set designer Mark Fisher, who began working with Waters on the concept for the stage show during the recording of the album. His production involved 420 cardboard bricks that, over the course of the first half of the show, would create a wall measuring 31-feet high and 160-feet wide in front of the band.

For the second half, animation provided by Gerald Scarfe, whose artwork was integral to the album's design, would be projected onto the wall, which would come crashing down in the finale. The idea of not being seen by the audience was unprecedented for a band but Waters was adamant that it reflect the main character's alienation from society.

The production included huge inflatable puppets — also designed by Scarfe — representing several characters, including a massive mother figure and an evil-looking teacher that loomed over the wall and walked across the stage. Two props from previous tours were included – the famous flying pig in 'Run Like Hell' and a model plane that crashed into the stage during 'In the Flesh?' There was a four-piece surrogate Floyd band who wore Pink Floyd masks. This 'tribute' band comprising of Snowy White (guitar), Andy Bown (bass), Willie Wilson (drums) and Peter Wood (keyboards), were used to recreate the complex arrangements from the record. A quartet of backing vocalists were also hired. The sound system was arguably the best they'd ever had on tour. Extra speaker cabinets under the tiered seating accentuated the rumbling collapse of the wall as the show reached its grand finale – giving the impression that the entire arena was crumbling.

Pink Floyd had originally intended to film the concerts at London's Earls Court for inclusion in Alan Parker's later film adaptation of the album.

'The '81 shows were put on for the film, but by the time we got to do them they'd already decided they didn't want to use very much,' David Gilmour said 20 years later. *'About 20 minutes were shot. For example, "Hey You" where the camera was*

Roger Waters, Dave Gilmour, Nick Mason, Rick Wright walking off stage at The Wall Concert, Earls Court, 1981

behind the wall focusing on us, then it went up and over the wall onto the audience. That's a great bit of footage. But only three tracks were filmed.'

The reviews were impressive.

'"The Wall" show remains a milestone in rock history and there's no point in denying it,' reported The New York Times. *'Never again will one be able to accept the technical clumsiness, distorted sound and meagre visuals of most arena rock concerts as inevitable. "The Wall" show will be the touchstone against which all future rock spectacles must be measured.'*

While 'Sounds' wrote: *'If "The Wall" turns out to be Pink Floyd's epitaph, they've bowed out with a grandiose, impressive, overblown and provocative spectacle.'*

Back stage, however, relations between Gilmour, Mason, Waters and Richard Wright were at an all-time low. Their four Winnebagos were parked in a circle with the doors facing away from the centre. An increasingly isolated Waters used his own vehicle to arrive at each venue and stayed in separate hotels from Gilmour, Mason and Wright. Despite having left the band upon completion of the album, Wright ended up being the only member of the group who made any money from the venture as a salaried session player.

'I just decided I'd go out and play my best,' he said. *'Possibly with the hope that, if it worked out, Waters' decision to have me out could have been reverted.'*

It did work out but there was no olive-branch extended to Wright by Waters. By the time the band played the final show of 'The Wall" tour in London on June 17 1981, the spectacular was well-honed. But Gilmour, Mason, Waters and Wright would not play again together for another 24 years. . .

1980

‘The problem, really, with the show is that it wasn’t a touring show’

Nick Mason

7 Feb	Los Angeles Memorial Sports Arena, LA, CA, USA
8 Feb	Los Angeles Memorial Sports Arena, LA, CA, USA
9 Feb	Los Angeles Memorial Sports Arena, LA, CA, USA
10 Feb	Los Angeles Memorial Sports Arena, LA, CA, USA
11 Feb	Los Angeles Memorial Sports Arena, LA, CA, USA
12 Feb	Los Angeles Memorial Sports Arena, LA, CA, USA
13 Feb	Los Angeles Memorial Sports Arena, LA, CA, USA
24 Feb	Nassau Veterans Memorial Coliseum, Uniondale, Long Island, NY, USA
25 Feb	Nassau Veterans Memorial Coliseum, Uniondale, Long Island, NY, USA
26 Feb	Nassau Veterans Memorial Coliseum, Uniondale, Long Island, NY, USA
27 Feb	Nassau Veterans Memorial Coliseum, Uniondale, Long Island, NY, USA
28 Feb	Nassau Veterans Memorial Coliseum, Uniondale, Long Island, NY, USA
4 Aug	Earls Court Exhibition Hall, London, England
5 Aug	Earls Court Exhibition Hall, London, England
6 Aug	Earls Court Exhibition Hall, London, England
7 Aug	Earls Court Exhibition Hall, London, England
8 Aug	Earls Court Exhibition Hall, London, England
9 Aug	Earls Court Exhibition Hall, London, England

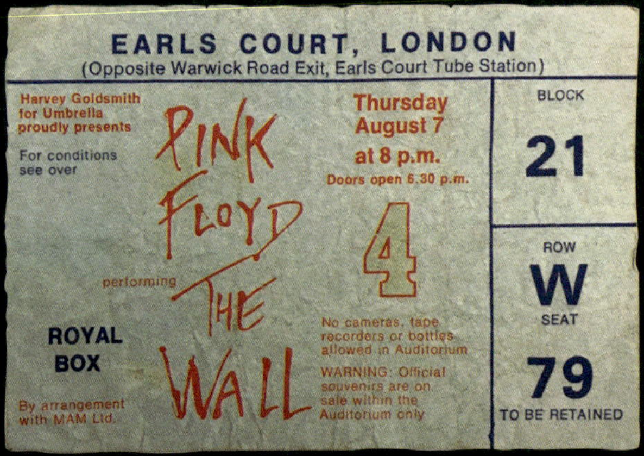

15 Feb Westfalenhalle, Dortmund, West Germany
16 Feb Westfalenhalle, Dortmund, West Germany
17 Feb Westfalenhalle, Dortmund, West Germany
18 Feb Westfalenhalle, Dortmund, West Germany
19 Feb Westfalenhalle, Dortmund, West Germany

14 Jun Earls Court Exhibition Hall, London, England
15 Jun Earls Court Exhibition Hall, London, England
16 Jun Earls Court Exhibition Hall, London, England
17 Jun Earls Court Exhibition Hall, London, England

Typical set list:

In the FleshThe Thin IceAnother Brick in the Wall, Part OneThe Happiest Days of Our LivesAnother Brick in the Wall, Part TwoMotherGoodbye Blue SkyWhat Shall We Do Now?Empty SpacesYoung LustOne of My TurnsDon't Leave Me NowAnother Brick in the Wall, Part Three)The Last Few BricksGoodbye Cruel WorldHey YouIs There Anybody Out There?Nobody HomeVeraBring The Boys Back HomeComfortably NumbThe Show Must Go OnIn The Flesh?Run Like HellWaiting for the WormsThe TrialOutside

PINK
FLOYD
THE WALL

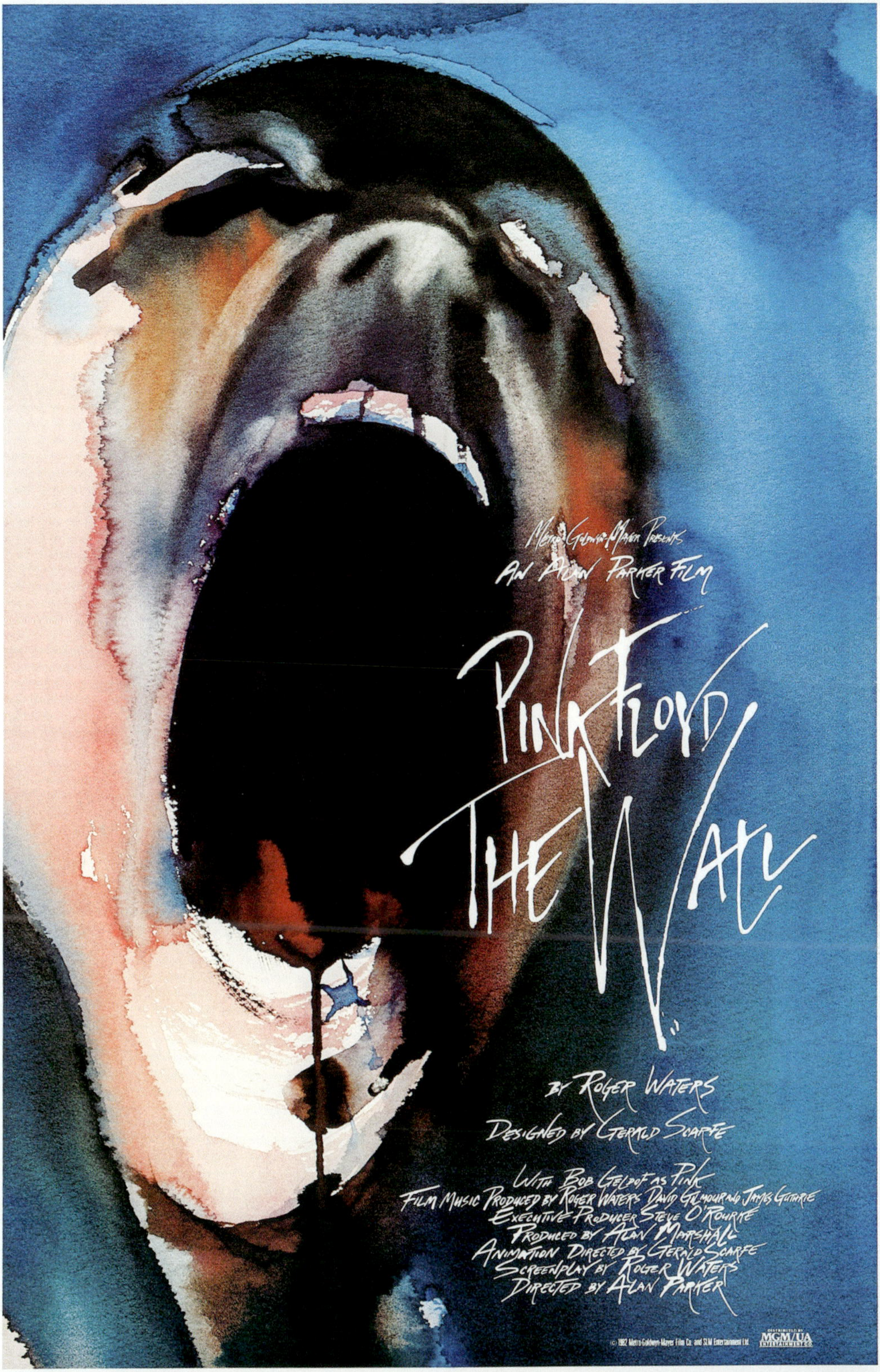
METRO-GOLDWYN-MAYER PRESENTS
AN ALAN PARKER FILM
PINK FLOYD
THE WALL
BY ROGER WATERS
DESIGNED BY GERALD SCARFE
WITH BOB GELDOF AS PINK
FILM MUSIC PRODUCED BY ROGER WATERS DAVID GILMOUR AND JAMES GUTHRIE
EXECUTIVE PRODUCER STEVE O'ROURKE
PRODUCED BY ALAN MARSHALL
ANIMATION DIRECTED BY GERALD SCARFE
SCREENPLAY BY ROGER WATERS
DIRECTED BY ALAN PARKER
(c) 1982 Metro-Goldwyn-Mayer Film Co. and SLM Entertainment Ltd.
DISTRIBUTED BY MGM/UA ENTERTAINMENT CO.

AND THEN THERE WERE THREE

'Pink Floyd are alive and well and recording in England'

Statement put out by David Gilmour and Nick Mason in 1986

After two further years of in-fighting and the release of forgettable-but-aptly named album, 'The Final Cut', Roger Waters formally left Floyd in 1985, firmly believing the band would not continue without him. However, Gilmour and Mason were determined to carry on as Pink Floyd. Waters threatened legal action against Gilmour and Mason, as well as any promoters who deigned to put on these shows as Pink Floyd concerts. However, by 1987, a settlement had been reached with Waters agreeing to drop his High Court action. Relations between the two factions were fraught to say the least. In short, there were none beyond their respective lawyers' offices – and wouldn't be for the next 18 years. Waters launched a solo career but time proved he couldn't compete with the juggernaut that was Floyd.

The 'Momentary Lapse of Reason' album, penned by Gilmour, was released in early September 1987. He had abandoned the idea of writing another 'concept' work in favour of a more conventional approach and with the album's release was hungry to tour. Ditto Mason and, also, Rick Wright, who was invited to join the tour, although legalities prevented him from re-joining the band officially. For some time, it was touch-and-go as to whether the tour would go ahead due to a question of finance and sponsorship.

'Since the early '80s, sponsorship had become a major element in tour financing but, although attractive, this was not an option that was available for us,' Nick Mason later explained. *'With all the unknown elements facing our reception – and the potential of a dramatic pratfall – there was no queue of cola or trainer shoe manufacturers outside the door. We couldn't put all the tickets on sale and use the money up front. The only viable way to do it was to have me and Dave fork out. In my particular case, I was a bit short of ready cash for the millions required, so I eventually went down to the upmarket equivalent of a pawn shop and hocked my 1962 GTO Ferrari – probably my most prized possession – but it meant I had little trouble financing my half of the tour set-up costs.'*

A group of youthful session musicians was assembled – Guy Pratt (Bass), Gary Wallis (Percussion), Tim Renwick (Guitar), Jon Carin (Keyboards), Scott Page (Saxophone), and Rachel Fury, Margaret Taylor (later replaced by Lorelei McBroom) and Durga McBroom as backing singers. It took some time to 'whip' this new-look Floyd into stage-ready shape.
'It was a disaster to begin with,' said Tim Renwick. *'Nobody could remember how to play anything. It was desperate.'*

After four weeks of intense rehearsals in Canada, they were deemed ready. The stage-show and SVX also required a considerable amount of prep. In the six years since Floyd had toured 'The Wall', stage, sound and lighting technology had moved on in leaps and bounds. However, this outing still included such

Pink Floyd pose backstage at the Rosemont Horizon during the band's A Momentary Lapse of Reason Tour on September 28, 1987

Floyd staging classics as a giant circular screen onto which was projected vintage and newly commissioned footage, the mirror ball, the ubiquitous flying hog, the crashing model plane – which would be replaced during the tour with a crashing bed – and myriad lasers and lights. New elements included a wondrous, winged inflatable figure that 'flew' above the audience and stage in 'Learning to Fly, 'pods' of light and dry-ice machines positioned on tracks above the stage, and four smaller light units, known collectively as 'Floyd Droids' and individually as 'Manny', 'Moe', 'Jack' and 'Cloyd', which ascended from the stage to illuminate the audience at suitable intervals. Two hundred and forty units made up the quadraphonic speaker system. It was, as was to be expected from Pink Floyd, a truly sensational comeback.

'The atmosphere before the first show in Ottawa was electric,' Nick Mason was to recall.

For some fans and reviewers, however, Roger Waters was missed – plus many only wanted to hear old favourites rather than new material from the new album.

'Pink Floyd opened its world tour before about 25000 fans Wednesday night with a multimedia extravaganza that soared

The album artwork for Pink Floyd's A Momentary Lapse of Reason, released in 1987

during the older songs but bogged down on new material that made the absence of Roger Waters glaringly obvious,' wrote 'Canadian Press, reviewing the opening night of the tour in Ottawa, Canada. *'The trio – augmented by a seven-member band – made no mention of Waters, who is on a solo tour and performing many Floyd songs. As an entertainment, it was a vintage spectacular, a comfortably numb experience enhanced by visual treats. For its first public performance in years and first without Waters, the band trotted out many of their favourite tricks from the 1970s like the giant inflated pig. And the plane – a replica flew around the football stadium on a guide wire and crashed beside the mammoth stage. Lighting modules descended from the ceiling like flying saucers. Voices and sound effects made heads turn sharply at the back of the stadium where additional speakers were set up as part of the quadraphonic sound system. But the band needs help. Except for Gilmour, none of the musicians displayed much flash and almost everyone stands still. Many new songs are best described as droning dirges where the excitement is waiting for the monumental chord change. During the hour-long opening set, the aisles were busy with bored fans. Clearly everyone was waiting for the old stuff. It mesmerised those fans who consider a Pink Floyd concert the ultimate concert experience – especially on various recreational and industrial strength drugs. In*

the end, the band delivered just what the fans wanted. Pink Floyd is no longer a leading creative entity, but as entertainment, a Floyd concert is still an aural and visual treat that any rock fans shouldn't miss.'

Going into 1988, Floyd toured New Zealand, Australia and Japan before heading back to North America from April to June. Then it was on to Europe where they performed at the historic Versailles Palace near Paris at the end of that month in addition to several dates in Denmark, Norway, Switzerland, the UK and Ireland. In mid-August, they returned to the US where they continued touring until the end of the month. Taking a break from touring, Floyd reconvened to go back on the road in spring 1989 with concerts in Belgium, France, Italy – most notably on a barge moored off St Mark's Square in Venice, Scandinavia, Austria, Germany, the UK, and, for the first time, Russia. The final show took place in Marseille, France on July 18 1989, almost 18 months since they'd played their first gig of the tour in Ottawa.

Performing live onstage on Another Lapse Tour, 1989

'It was over the top large,' remembers guitarist Tim Renwick, *'and I had started to feel like a pretty small cog in it. On the last week you'd be introduced to people you'd already been around the world with. You lived in this bubble. Back home, taking out the trash was a chore. I came down to earth with a bump.'*

It had been a phenomenally successful year-and-a-half. Grossing US$135 million and playing to a total of 5.5 million people, the 'Momentary Lapse of Reason' tour was lauded as one of the best live shows in rock history. It had also been a positive experience for band and crew alike with even the reticent Rick Wright declaring it to be the happiest tour he had ever been part of. An add-on appearance at a charity event at Knebworth in September 1990 in inclement weather did little to dampen their spirits. Floyd, *sans* Waters, were well and truly back – and bigger than they'd ever been. . .

1987

A Momentary Lapse of Reason USA & Canada Tour 1st leg

'We wanted to be world conquering. We wanted to leave no one in any doubt that we meant business'

David Gilmour

Typical set list:

Shine On You Crazy Diamond
Signs of Life
Learning to Fly
Yet Another Movie
Round and Around
A New Machine, Part 1
Terminal Frost
A New Machine, Part 2
Sorrow
The Dogs of War
On The Turning Away
One of These Days
Time
The Great Gig In The Sky
Wish You Were Here
Welcome To The Machine
Us And Them
Money
Another Brick In The Wall, Part 2
Comfortably Numb
One Slip
Run Like Hell

Sep 9 Ottawa, Canada – Lansdowne Park
Sep 12 Montreal, Canada – Montreal Forum
Sep 13 Montreal, Canada – Montreal Forum
Sep 14 Montreal, Canada – Montreal Forum
Sep 16 Cleveland, USA – Municipal Stadium
Sep 17 Cleveland, USA – Municipal Stadium
Sep 19 Philadelphia, USA – JFK Stadium
Sep 21 Toronto, Canada – CNE Stadium
Sep 22 Toronto, Canada – CNE Stadium
Sep 23 Toronto, Canada – CNE Stadium
Sep 25 Rosemont, USA – Rosemont Horizon
Sep 26 Rosemont, USA – Rosemont Horizon
Sep 27 Rosemont, USA – Rosemont Horizon
Sep 28 Rosemont, USA – Rosemont Horizon
Sep 30 Milwaukee, USA – County Stadium
Oct 3 Syracuse, USA – Carrier Dome
Oct 5 New York, USA – Madison Square Garden
Oct 6 New York, USA – Madison Square Garden
Oct 7 New York, USA – Madison Square Garden
Oct 10 East Rutherford, USA – Brendan Byrne Arena
Oct 11 East Rutherford, USA – Brendan Byrne Arena
Oct 12 East Rutherford, USA – Brendan Byrne Arena
Oct 14 Hartford, USA – Hartford Civic Center
Oct 15 Hartford, USA – Hartford Civic Center
Oct 16 Providence, USA – Providence Civic Center
Oct 17 Providence, USA – Providence Civic Center
Oct 19 Landover, USA – Capital Center
Oct 20 Landover, USA – Capital Center
Oct 21 Landover, USA – Capital Center
Oct 22 Landover, USA – Capital Center
Oct 25 Chapel Hill, USA – Dean Smith Center
Oct 26 Chapel Hill, USA – Dean Smith Center
Oct 30 Tampa, USA – Tampa Stadium
Nov 1 Miami, USA – Miami Orange Bowl
Nov 3 Atlanta, USA – Omni Coliseum
Nov 4 Atlanta, USA – Omni Coliseum
Nov 5 Atlanta, USA – Omni Coliseum
Nov 7 Lexington, USA – Rupp Arena
Nov 8 Lexington, USA – Rupp Arena
Nov 10 Pontiac, USA – Pontiac Silverdome
Nov 12 Indianapolis, USA – Hoosier Dome
Nov 15 St. Louis, USA – St. Louis Arena
Nov 16 St. Louis, USA – St. Louis Arena
Nov 18 Houston, USA – Astrodome
Nov 19 Austin, USA – Frank Erwin Center
Nov 20 Austin, USA – Frank Erwin Center
Nov 21 Dallas, USA – Reunion Arena
Nov 22 Dallas, USA – Reunion Arena
Nov 23 Dallas, USA – Reunion Arena
Nov 26 Los Angeles, USA – Los Angeles Memorial Sports Arena
Nov 27 Los Angeles, USA – Los Angeles Memorial Sports Arena
Nov 28 Los Angeles, USA – Los Angeles Memorial Sports Arena
Nov 30 Los Angeles, USA – Los Angeles Memorial Sports Arena
Dec 1 Los Angeles, USA – Los Angeles Memorial Sports Arena
Dec 3 Oakland, USA – Oakland-Alameda County Coliseum
Dec 4 Oakland, USA – Oakland-Alameda County Coliseum
Dec 5 Oakland, USA – Oakland-Alameda
Dec 6 Oakland, USA – Oakland-Alameda
Dec 8 Seattle, USA – Kingdome
Dec 10 Vancouver, Canada – BC Place Stadium

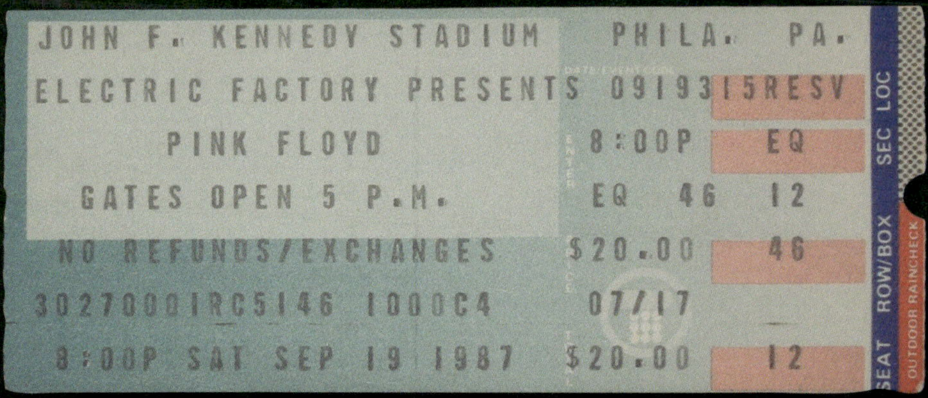

A Momentary Lapse of Reason Australia & New Zealand Tour

Jan 22 Auckland, New Zealand – Western Springs Stadium

Jan 27 Sydney, Australia – Sydney Entertainment Center

Jan 28 Sydney, Australia – Sydney Entertainment Center

Jan 29 Sydney, Australia – Sydney Entertainment Center

Jan 30 Sydney, Australia – Sydney Entertainment Center

Jan 31 Sydney, Australia – Sydney Entertainment Center

Feb 1 Sydney, Australia – Sydney Entertainment Center

Feb 2 Sydney, Australia – Sydney Entertainment Center

Feb 3 Sydney, Australia – Sydney Entertainment Center

Feb 4 Sydney, Australia – Sydney Entertainment Center

Feb 5 Sydney, Australia – Sydney Entertainment Center

Feb 7 Brisbane, Australia – Brisbane Entertainment Center

Feb 8 Brisbane, Australia – Brisbane Entertainment Center

Feb 11 Adelaide, Australia – Thebarton Oval

Feb 13 Melbourne, Australia – Melbourne & Olympic Parks

Feb 14 Melbourne, Australia – Melbourne & Olympic Parks

Feb 15 Melbourne, Australia – Melbourne & Olympic Parks

Feb 16 Melbourne, Australia – Melbourne & Olympic Parks

Feb 17 Melbourne, Australia – Melbourne & Olympic Parks

Feb 18 Melbourne, Australia – Melbourne & Olympic Parks

Feb 19 Melbourne, Australia – Melbourne & Olympic Parks

Feb 20 Melbourne, Australia – Melbourne & Olympic Parks

Feb 24 Perth, Australia – East Frenmantle Oval

A Momentary Lapse of Reason Japan Tour

Mar 2 Tokyo, Japan – Budokan

Mar 3 Tokyo, Japan – Budokan

Mar 4 Tokyo, Japan – Yoyogi Olympic Pool

Mar 5 Tokyo, Japan – Yoyogi Olympic Pool

Mar 6 Tokyo, Japan – Yoyogi Olymic Pool

Mar 8 Osaka, Japan – Osaka-jo Hall

Mar 9 Osaka, Japan – Osaka-jo Hall

Mar 11 Nagoya, Japan – Rainbow Hall

A Momentary Lapse of Reason USA & Canada Tour – 2nd leg

Apr 15 Los Angeles, USA – Los Angeles Memorial Coliseum

Apr 18 Denver, USA – Mile High Stadium

Apr 20 Sacramento, USA – Charles C. Hughes Stadium

Apr 22 Oakland, USA – Oakland-Alameda County Coliseum

Apr 23 Oakland, USA – Oakland-Alameda County Coliseum

Apr 28 Irving, USA – Texas Stadium

Apr 30 Orlando, USA – Citrus Bowl

May 4 Raleigh, USA – Carter-Finley Stadium

May 6 Foxboro, USA – Sullivan Stadium

May 8 Foxboro, USA – Sullivan Stadium

May 11 Montreal, Canada – Olympic Stadium

May 13 Toronto, Canada – CNE Stadium

May 15 Philadelphia, USA – Veterans Stadium

May 17 Philadelphia, USA – Veterans Stadium

May 18 Cedar Falls, USA – UNI-Dome

May 20 Madison, USA – Camp Randall Stadium

May 21 Rosemont, USA – Rosemont Horizon

May 22 Rosemont, USA – Rosemont Horizon

May 24 Minneapolis, USA – Hubert H. Humphrey Metrodome

May 26 Kansas City, USA – Arrowhead Stadium

May 28 Columbus, USA – Ohio Stadium

May 30 Pittsburgh, USA – Three Rivers Stadium

Jun 1 Washington, USA – RFK Stadium

Jun 3 East Rutherford, USA – Giants Stadium

Jun 4 East Rutherford, USA – Giants Stadium

1988 A Momentary Lapse of Reason Europe Tour – 1st leg

Jun 10 Nantes, France – Stade de La Beaujoire

Jun 13 Rotterdam, Netherlands – Feijenoord Stadion

Jun 14 Rotterdam, Netherlands – Feijenoord Stadion

Jun 16 Berlin, Germany – Reichstagsgelande

Jun 18 Mannheim, Germany – Reichstagsgelande

Jun 21 Versailles, France – Place d'Armes du Chateau de Versailles

Jun 22 Versailles, France – Place d'Armes du Chateau de Versailles

Jun 25 Hanover, Germany – Niedersachsenstadion

Jun 27 Dortmund, Germany – Westfalenhalle

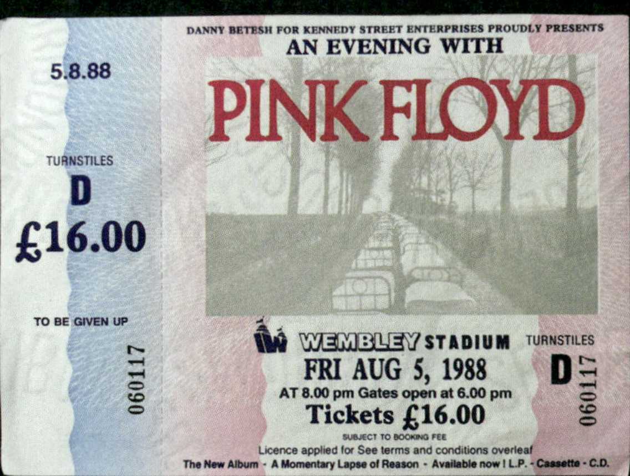

Jun 28 Dortmund, Germany – Westfalenhalle

Jun 29 Dortmund, Germany – Westfalenhalle

Jul 1 Vienna, Austria – Ernst-Happel-Stadion

Jul 3 Munich, Germany – Olympiastadion

Jul 6 Torino, Italy – Stadio Olimpico di Torino

Jul 8 Modena, Italy – Stadio Alberto Braglia

Jul 9 Modena, Italy – Stadio Alberto Braglia

Jul 11 Rome, Italy – Stadio Flaminio

Jul 12 Rome, Italy – Stadio Flaminio

Jul 15 Grenoble, France – Stade du Municipal

Jul 17 Nice, France – Stade Charles-Ehrmann

Jul 20 Barcelona, Spain – Estadi de Sarriá

Jul 22 Madrid, Spain – Estadioo Vicente Calderón

Jul 24 Montpellier, France – Espace Richter

Jul 26 Basel, Switzerland – Füssballstadion

Jul 28 Lille, France – Stadium Nord

Jul 31 Copenhagen, Denmark – Gentofte Stadion

Aug 2 Oslo, Norway – Valle Hovin

Aug 5 London, UK – Wembley Arena

Aug 6 London, UK – Wembley Arena

Aug 8 Manchester, UK – Maine Road

1988 A Momentary Lapse of Reason USA Tour – 3rd leg

Aug 12 Cleveland, USA – Richfield Coliseum

Aug 13 Cleveland, USA – Richfield Coliseum

Aug 14 Cleveland, USA – Richfield Coliseum

Aug 16 Auburn Hills, USA – The Palace of Auburn Hills

Aug 17 Auburn Hills, USA – The Palace of Auburn Hills

Aug 19 Uniondale, USA – Nassau Coliseum

Aug 20 Uniondale, USA – Nassau Coliseum

Aug 21 Uniondale, USA – Nassau Coliseum

Aug 22 Uniondale, USA – Nassau Coliseum

Aug 23 Uniondale, USA – Nassau Coliseum

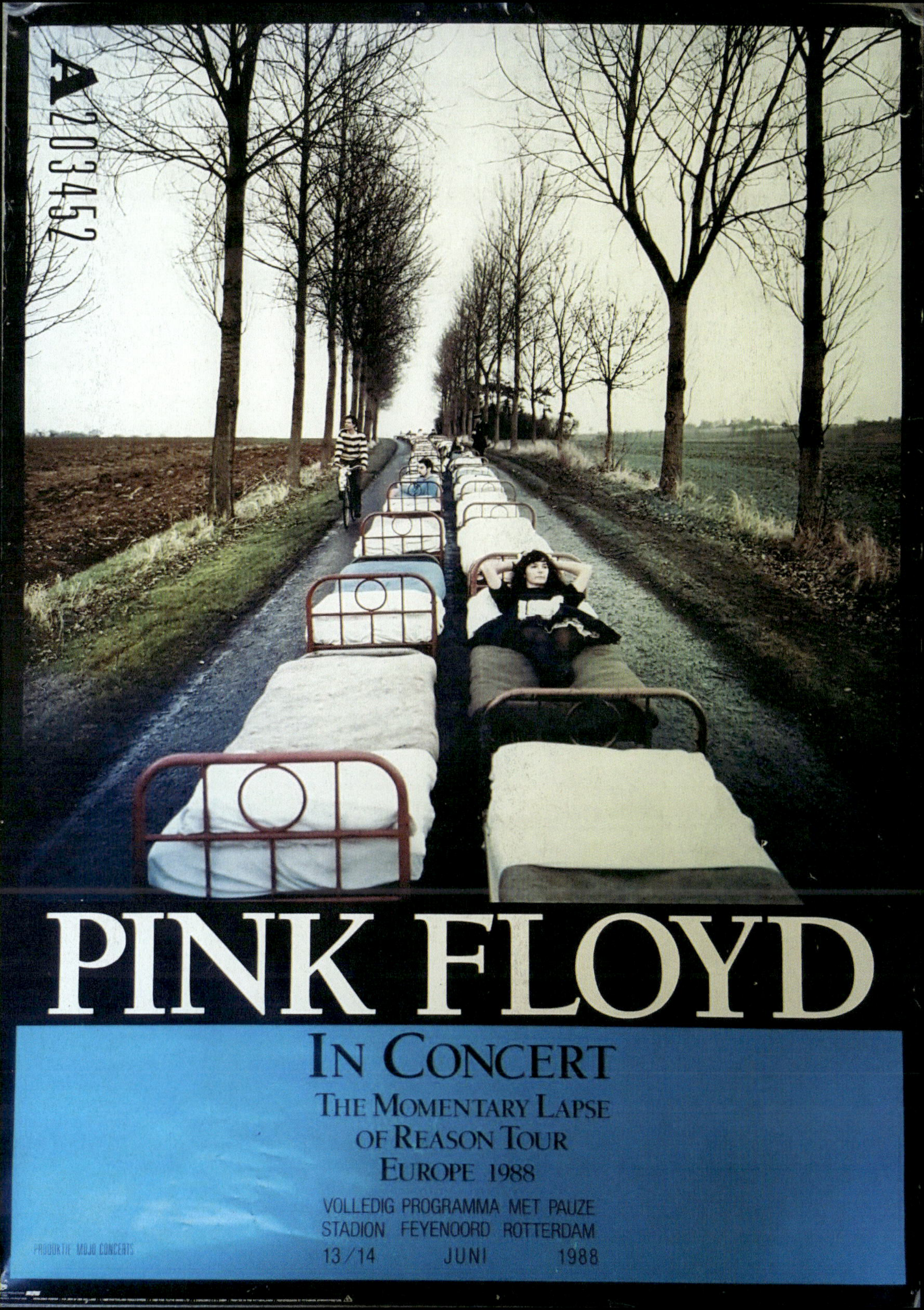
A 203452
PINK FLOYD
IN CONCERT
THE MOMENTARY LAPSE
OF REASON TOUR
EUROPE 1988
VOLLEDIG PROGRAMMA MET PAUZE
STADION FEYENOORD ROTTERDAM
13/14 JUNI 1988
PRODUKTIE MOJO CONCERTS

THE MOMENTARY LAPSE OF REASON TOUR
PINK FLOYD
IN CONCERT
POR PRIMERA VEZ EN ESPAÑA
EL AUTENTICO SONIDO CUADRAFONICO
RECOMENDADO POR
LOS 40 PRINCIPALES
ULTIMO DISCO A LA VENTA
"A MOMENTARY LAPSE OF REASON"
EN DISCOS EMI
Ayuntamiento de Madrid
VIERNES 22 JULIO A LAS 21,30 HORAS
ESTADIO VICENTE CALDERON
VENTA ANTICIPADA DE LOCALIDADES: DISCOPLAY, LOS SOTANOS, Gran Via 55, La Vaguada y Fco. Sancha; PUB HONDIGAÑO, Espinar y Carabanchel; PUB VK, Puerto de Canfran 14; DISTRITO 18, Cordillera de Cuera 19, Vallecas; PUB KOMITTE, Silva 6; PUB EL TORITO, Pelayo; PUC CROSS, Dr. Bellido 23. LA ORGANIZACION NO SE RESPONSABILIZA DE LA AUTENTICIDAD DE LAS LOCALIDADES SI NO SON ADQUIRIDAS EN LOS PUNTOS OFICIALES
PARA MAS INFORMACION TEL.91-729 2499 DE 9A 18H.
J.R. GUZMAN

LESLY PRESENTE
PINK FLOYD
IN
CONCERT
PARIS/BERCY
MARDI 27 JUIN 1989
A 20H30
LA CINQ 5
NRJ
La plus belle radio
180 F
Nº 015141

FRANTOMASI
20 MAGGIO 1989 - MONZA/AUTODROMO
posto unico
Nº 35660
ANOTHER LAPSE
TUTTO
PINK FLOYD
IN CONCERT

1989

A Momentary Lapse of Reason Europe Tour 2nd leg

May 13	Werchter, Belgium – Rock Werchter Festival
May 16	Verona, Italy – Verona Arena
May 17	Verona, Italy – Verona Arena
May 18	Verona, Italy – Verona Arena
May 20	Monza, Italy – Arena Concerti
May 22	Livorno, Italy – Stadio Comunale Ardenza
May 23	Livorno, Italy – Stadio Comunale Ardenza
May 25	Cava Dei Tirreni, Italy – Stadio Simonetta Lamberti
May 26	Cava Dei Tirreni, Italy – Stadio Simonetta Lamberti
May 31	Athens, Greece – Olympic Stadium
Jun 3	Moscow, Russia – Olympic Stadium
Jun 4	Moscow, Russia – Olympic Stadium
Jun 6	Moscow, Russia – Olympic Stadium
Jun 7	Moscow, Russia – Olympic Stadium
Jun 8	Moscow, Russia – Olympic Stadium
Jun 10	Lahti, Finland – Lahden Suurhalli
Jun 12	Stockholm, Sweden – Globen
Jun 13	Stockholm, Sweden – Globen
Jun 14	Stockholm, Sweden – Globen
Jun 16	Hamburg, Germany – Festwiesse Im Stadtpark
Jun 18	Cologne, Germany – Mungersdorfer Stadion
Jun 20	Frankfurt, Germany – Festhalle Frankfurt
Jun 21	Frankfurt, Germany – Festhalle Frankfurt
Jun 23	Linz, Austria – Linzer Stadion
Jun 25	Stuttgart, Germany – Neckarstadion
Jun 27	Paris, France – Palais Omnisports de Paris-Bercy
Jun 28	Paris, France – Palais Omnisports de Paris-Bercy
Jun 29	Paris, France – Palais Omnisports de Paris-Bercy
Jun 30	Paris, France – Palais Omnisports de Paris-Bercy
Jul 1	Paris, France – Palais Omnisports de Paris-Bercy
Jul 4	London, UK – London Arena
Jul 5	London, UK – London Arena
Jul 6	London, UK – London Arena
Jul 7	London, UK – London Arena
Jul 8	London, UK – London Arena
Jul 9	London, UK – London Arena
Jul 10	Nijmegen, Netherlands – Goffertpark
Jul 12	Lausanne, Switzerland – Stade Olympique de la Pontaise
Jul 15	Venice, Italy – Grand Canal
Jul 18	Marseille, France – Stade Vélodrome

THE DIVISION BELL TOUR

'There are eight caterers on the tour; they cook dinner for 220 people on show nights. They bake 20 loaves of bread in an afternoon, get through 400 pints of milk, 1000 eggs, 1200 tea bags, 1000 cans of soft drinks, 25 boxes of cornflakes and two boxes of Romaine lettuce – this last for the Floyd's favourite Caesar salad. Special supplies of Marmite, Weetabix, Branston Pickle, marmalade, English mustard and Earl Grey tea-bags are shipped out from England at regular intervals'

Catering arrangements on The Division Bell Tour.

They may not have known it at the time but 'Division Bell' was the final concert tour by Pink Floyd. Gilmour, Mason and Wright, who had officially become a full member of the band again when legal issues had been ironed out during the recording of the album of the same name. They went back out on the road in late March 1994 – two days after the release of the album which cruised to the top of the charts in both the UK and the US.

The concerts featured even more impressive special effects than the previous tour. *'Bigger! Better! More!'* was the mantra. These SFX included two custom designed airships, two giant pigs, 300 speakers, a 40-foot circular projection screen and two pulse lasers. Three stages leapfrogged around North America and Europe, each 180 feet long and featuring a 130-foot arch resembling the Hollywood Bowl venue. All in all, the tour required 700 tons of steel carried by 53 articulated trucks, a crew of 161 people and an initial investment of US$4 million plus US$25 million of running costs just to stage. For this tour Floyd were using extremely powerful, isotope-splitting copper-vapour lasers. These gold-coloured lasers were worth over $120,000 apiece and previously had only been used in nuclear research and high-speed photography. However, the band also played homage to their past by commissioning original lighting engineer Peter Wynne-Wilson to re-create liquid and oil, psychedelic patterns – and updated versions of 'The Daleks' – to 'shine on' while Floyd played the opening number of this tour, the Barrett classic 'Astronomy Domine'. This was the first time it had been played live for decades.

The set was a throwback to other familiar Pink Floyd themes with new projection films created by another old comrade

Pink Floyd in concert in Chantilly, France on July 31, 1994

Storm Thorgerson to accompany 'Money', 'Time' and 'Shine On You Crazy Diamond'. The massive, face-to-face Division Bell monoliths created for the tour would go down in Floyd lore as some of the bands most enduring images. Joining the 'core' Floyd combo again on stage were Jon Carin, Tim Renwick, Guy Pratt, Gary Wallis and Durga McBroom, along with newbie singers, Sam Brown and Claudia Fontaine. Their old saxophonist Dick Parry also 're-joined', replacing Scott Page. While preparing for the tour, this extended Pink Floyd spent most of March rehearsing in a hanger at Norton Air Force Base in California. The 'Division Bell' tour opened on March 29 at the Joe Robbie Stadium in Miami and rolled on through the US through spring and summer. A heavy rainfall brought proceedings to an abrupt end in Houston, causing the show to be abandoned due to safety issues. Things weren't exactly sunny on stage, either, as Gilmour, Mason and Wright had decided to take the first bow alone at the close of each show.

'The positive spirit, Dave, Rick and I were enjoying threatened to dilute the overall team theme and certainly changed the dynamic,' Nick Mason was to say in retrospect.

On July 15, Floyd changed their set at the Pontiac Silverdrome in Detroit and for the second half of the show, performed the entire 'Dark Side of the Moon' for the first time since playing at Knebworth in July 1975.

'It was an emotional experience,' remembers Mason. *'It reminded me of our history, the way we were in 1973. That had made us a big band in America. But we reached a new plateau and immediately suffered for it from not knowing what to do next. The band disagreements, which never existed before, started then.'*

Pink Floyd at Olympic Stadium, Munich, Germany, 1994

The tour reached Europe in late July, opening with two gigs in Lisbon, Portugal.

'You cannot begin to imagine,' extolled the Melody Maker's review of the second show. *'I'm talking about scene and spectacle. About time and place. About the most expensive stadium show since wherever the last one was. . . 70,000 people were there and another 70,000 the previous night. What is it about Pink Floyd that ensures, wherever they go, multitudes will assemble to worshipfully watch them? Do they fill Antarctic arenas with dizzy, cheering penguins? But I understand. Pink Floyd today might be trademark, a cipher, a hologram of a band who never quite captured the spirit of the 'Times' in the first place but I understand. I understand because they open with 'Shine On Your Crazy Diamond' which I still hold to be one of the most perfect and beautiful pieces of music ever written, and they perform it on the scale of the fall of Rome. You don't even have to watch the band. Floyd's old circular screen rises above the filament (yes, the Planetarium slides are back, too), but now it's huge, 40 feet across, circled with spotlights – engorged, basically, with enormous amounts of cash – and an allegorical film by Storm Thorgerson plays upon it. . . David Gilmour has re-assembled a Pink Floyd which is more of a showband than a rock n roll group. To even consider it in terms of rock n roll is to miss the point. Pink Floyd belongs in the same league as 'Holiday on Ice' – massive, mythic, meticulous showbiz, an orgy of stupendous and silly SFX. I have become un 'Comfortably Numb', when, at the climax, the very metaphor presents itself in the form of the world's largest revolving mirrored disco ball. It then transforms into the world's largest electric palm tree. The show is no less than the exultant culmination of three decades of hi-tech kitsch.'*

An unexpected olive branch was extended to Roger Waters as the tour reached the UK that October. With the band due to play an unprecedented 14 nights at London's Earls Court, they invited Roger Waters to join them on stage for the 'Dark Side of the Moon'.

'I thought it would be a good thing for the fans,' David Gilmour was later to say. *'But also, it was with the safety cushion of knowing he wouldn't do it. It was a genuine offer, though.'*

Not unexpectedly, Waters declined, later denouncing *'the inherent betrayal'* of this Pink Floyd playing songs, especially from 'The Wall', in football stadiums and the like.

'There would have to be some other reason for me to stand on stage with Dave Gilmour and play Dark Side of the Moon,' he said. *'There's too much history.'*

On the first night of the Earls Court dates on 12 October, a 1200-capacity stand collapsed, sounding, according to Nick Mason, *'like a roll of thunder'*. Ninety-six people were injured, with 36 needing hospital treatment. Six were detained overnight with back, neck and rib injuries, but all were expected to make a full recovery. The show was immediately cancelled and re-scheduled for October 17th, one of their rest days. The stand was replaced and all other shows went ahead as planned. Gilmour said afterwards: *'We are very distressed at what happened and we are particularly concerned about the injured. We are also sorry to have disappointed those who came to see the show.'* He later added: *'I am angry and upset about what happened... it is extremely fortunate nobody died. When the accident happened, I was at the back of the stage waiting to go on. I heard banging and presumed there was a fault on the PA system. We were about to start playing when the house lights came up. I was getting a bit frantic with people when someone said they were stopping the concert.'*

It had been previously agreed that proceeds from all the Earls Court shows would be shared out amongst various charities and Gilmour issued a statement assuring these bodies that the accident would not affect the monies they were due. That was not the end of the story, however. The re-scheduled concert saw traumatised fans sat in exactly the same seats they'd had on the first night – giving them even more cause for complaint as it was reported that Earls Court were not giving due attention to claims for compensation for damaged clothing, time off work and medical bills. One good thing about this re-scheduled show for those in Block Nine was that they were all given special t-shirts to 'commemorate' the incident and were all invited backstage after the show to meet the band.

The last word should go to Gilmour, who announced on the Earls Court stage, *'If I were you, I'd sue somebody. Er, not me, though...'*

During 'Wish You Were Here' on the last night of the Earls Court dates, the backing singers emerged dressed as cleaners and began sweeping the stage while some members of the band and crew donned plastic 'Groucho Marx' noses and glasses.

In all, the Division Bell tour played to 5.5 million people in 68 cities around the world, with each concert gathering an average audience of 45,000 fans. At the end of the year, it was announced as the biggest tour ever – for the time – with a worldwide gross of over £150 million (about US$250 million). In the U.S. alone, it grossed US$103.5 million from 59 concerts. To mark the tour and its success, a live album and video, both titled 'Pulse' were released. But it was very much the end of an era, spanning almost 30 years. On only one more, singular occasion would Pink Floyd play together again – and on that occasion Roger Waters would agree to join the band on stage. And David Gilmour would let him.

Original vinyl album cover for The Division Bell, 1994

PINK FLOYD • THE DIVISION BELL

1994

'Since they staked their financial future in the 'Momentary Lapse of Reason' album and tour six years ago, Gilmour and Mason have cleaned up, having successfully proved that Pink Floyd could not only continue to exist without Roger Waters, but that it could both subsume and transcend him, just as it had done with its first singer-songwriting front man Syd Barrett, many years previously'

Q Magazine

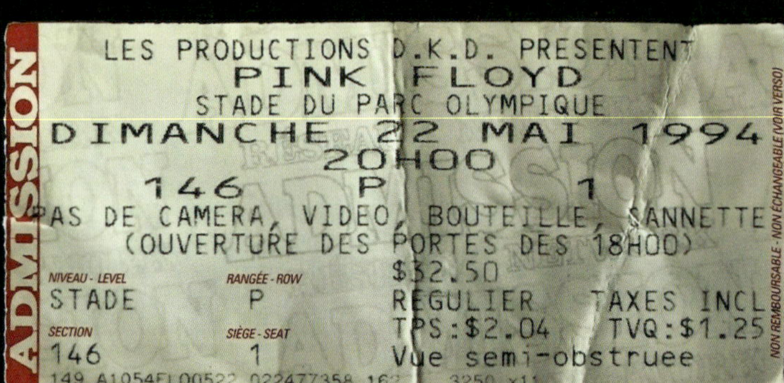

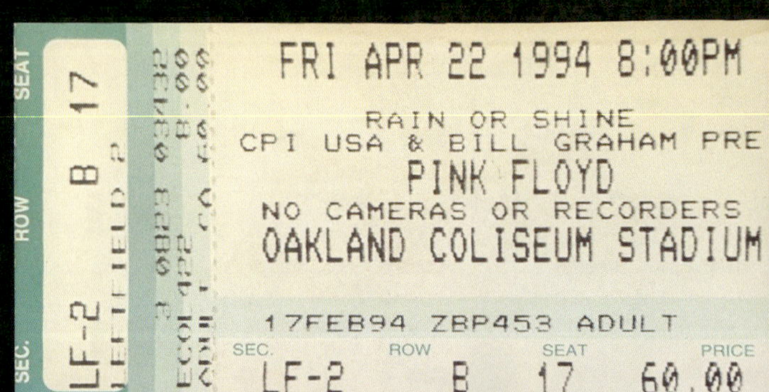

Typical set list March 30–July 14 1994:

Astronomy Domine Learning to Fly What Do You Want From Me On The Turning Away Take It Back A Great Day For Freedom Sorrow Keep Talking One of These Days Shine On You Crazy Diamond Breathe Time Breathe (reprise) High Hopes The Great Gig in the Sky Wish You Were Here Us and Them Money Another Brick in the Wall, Part 2 Comfortably Numb Hey You Run Like Hell

30 Mar	Joe Robbie Stadium, Miami, FL, USA
3 Apr	Alamo Dome, San Antonio, TX, USA
5 Apr	Rice University Stadium, Houston, TX, USA (show cut short due to weather)
9 Apr	Autodromo Hnos. Rodriguez, Mexico City, Mexico
10 Apr	Autodromo Hnos. Rodriguez, Mexico City, Mexico
14 Apr	Jack Murphy Stadium, San Diego, CA, USA
16 Apr	The Rose Bowl, Pasadena, Los Angeles, CA, USA
17 Apr	The Rose Bowl, Pasadena, Los Angeles, CA, USA
20 Apr	Oakland Coliseum Stadium, Oakland, CA, USA
21 Apr	Oakland Coliseum Stadium, Oakland, CA, USA
22 Apr	Oakland Coliseum Stadium, Oakland, CA, USA
24 Apr	Sun Devil Stadium, Tempe, AZ, USA
26 Apr	Sun Bowl Stadium, El Paso, TX, USA
28 Apr	Texas Stadium, Irving, Dallas, TX, USA
29 Apr	Texas Stadium, Irving, Dallas, TX, USA
1 May	Legion Field, Birmingham, AL, USA
3 May	Bobbie Dodd Stadium, Atlanta, GA, USA
4 May	Bobbie Dodd Stadium, Atlanta, GA, USA
6 May	Tampa Stadium, Tampa, FL, USA
8 May	Vanderbilt University Stadium, Nashville, TN, USA
10 May	Carter Finley Stadium, Raleigh, NC, USA
12 May	Death Valley Stadium, Clemson, SC, USA
14 May	Louisiana Superdrome, New Orleans, LA, USA
18 May	Foxboro Stadium, Foxboro, Boston, MA, USA
19 May	Foxboro Stadium, Foxboro, Boston, MA, USA
20 May	Foxboro Stadium, Foxboro, Boston, MA, USA
22 May	Stade du Parc Olympique, Montreal, Quebec, Canada
23 May	Stade du Parc Olympique, Montreal, Quebec, Canada
24 May	Stade du Parc Olympique, Montreal, Quebec, Canada
26 May	Municipal Stadium, Cleveland, OH, USA
27 May	Municipal Stadium, Cleveland, OH, USA
29 May	Ohio State University Stadium, Columbus, OH, USA
31 May	Three Rivers Stadium, Pittsburgh, PA, USA
2 Jun	Veterans Stadium, Philadelphia, PA, USA
3 Jun	Veterans Stadium, Philadelphia, PA, USA
4 Jun	Veterans Stadium, Philadelphia, PA, USA
6 Jun	Carrier Dome, Syracuse, NY, USA
10 Jun	Yankee Stadium, New York City, NY, USA
11 Jun	Yankee Stadium, New York City, NY, USA
14 Jun	Hoosier Dome, Indianapolis, IN, USA
16 Jun	Cyclone Stadium, Ames, IA, USA
18 Jun	Mile High Stadium, Denver, CO, USA
20 Jun	Arrowhead Stadium, Kansas City, MO, USA
22 Jun	Hubert H Humphrey Metrodome, Minneapolis, MN, USA
25 Jun	British Columbia Place Stadium, Vancouver, B.C., Canada

26 Jun	British Columbia Place Stadium, Vancouver, B.C., Canada
28 Jun	Commonwealth Stadium, Edmonton, Alberta, Canada
1 Jul	Winnipeg Stadium, Winnipeg, Manitoba, Canada
3 Jul	Camp Randall Stadium, Madison, WI, USA
5 Jul	Canadian National Exhibition Stadium, Toronto, Ontario, Canada
6 Jul	Canadian National Exhibition Stadium, Toronto, Ontario, Canada
7 Jul	Canadian National Exhibition Stadium, Toronto, Ontario, Canada
9 Jul	Robert F. Kennedy Stadium, Washington D.C, USA
10 Jul	Robert F. Kennedy Stadium, Washington D.C, USA
12 Jul	Soldier Field, Chicago, IL, USA
14 Jul	Pontiac Silverdome, Pontiac, MI, USA
15 Jul	Pontiac Silverdome, Pontiac, MI, USA
17 Jul	Giants Stadium, East Rutherford, NJ, USA

Typical set list July 15–October 29 1994:

Shine On You Crazy Diamond Learning to Fly High Hopes Coming Back to Life Take It Back Sorrow Keep Talking Another Brick in the Wall, Part 2 One of These Days The Dark Side of the Moon (entire album) Wish You Were Here Comfortably Numb Run Like Hell

18 Jul	Giants Stadium, East Rutherford, NJ, USA
22 Jul	Estadio de Alvalade, Lisbon, Portugal
23 Jul	Estadio de Alvalade, Lisbon, Portugal
25 Jul	Estadio Anoeta, San Sebastian, Spain
27 Jul	Estadio Olimpico, Barcelona, Spain
30 Jul	Chateau de Chantilly, Chantilly, France
31 Jul	Chateau de Chantilly, Chantilly, France
2 Aug	Mungersdorfer Stadion, Cologne, Germany
4 Aug	Olympiastadion, Munich, Germany
6 Aug	Fussballstadion St. Jakob, Basel, Switzerland
7 Aug	Fussballstadion St. Jakob, Basel, Switzerland
9 Aug	Amphitheatre du Chateau de Grammont, Montpellier, France
11 Aug	Esplanade des Quinconces, Bordeaux, France
13 Aug	Hockenheimring, Hockenheim, Germany
16 Aug	Niedersachsenstadion, Hannover, Germany
17 Aug	Niedersachsenstadion, Hannover, Germany
19 Aug	Wiener Neustadt-Flugfeld, Vienna, Austria
21 Aug	Maifeld am Olympiastadion, Berlin, Germany
23 Aug	Parkstadion, Gelsenkirchen, Germany
25 Aug	Parken, Copenhagen, Denmark
27 Aug	Ullevi Stadion, Gothenburg, Sweden
29 Aug	Valle Hovin Stadion, Oslo, Norway
30 Aug	Valle Hovin Stadion, Oslo, Norway
2 Sep	Festivalweide, Werchter, Belgium
3 Sep	Stadion Feyenoord, Rotterdam, The Netherlands
4 Sep	Stadion Feyenoord, Rotterdam, The Netherlands
5 Sep	Stadion Feyenoord, Rotterdam, The Netherlands
7 Sep	Strahov Stadion, Prague, Czech Republic
9 Sep	Stade de la Meinau, Strasbourg, France

11 Sep	Stade de Gerland, Lyon, France
13 Sep	Stadio delle Alpi, Torino, Italy
15 Sep	Stadio Friuli, Udine, Italy
17 Sep	Festa Nazionale dell'Unita, Modena, Italy
19 Sep	Studi di Cinecitta, Rome, Italy
20 Sep	Studi di Cinecitta, Rome, Italy
21 Sep	Studi di Cinecitta, Rome, Italy
23 Sep	Stade de Gerland, Lyon, France
25 Sep	Stade de la Pontaise, Lausanne, Switzerland
12 Oct	Earls Court Exhibition Hall, Earls Court, London, England (seat collapse forced abandonment of show)
13 Oct	Earls Court Exhibition Hall, London, England
14 Oct	Earls Court Exhibition Hall, London, England
15 Oct	Earls Court Exhibition Hall, London, England
16 Oct	Earls Court Exhibition Hall, London, England
17 Oct	Earls Court Exhibition Hall, London, England
19 Oct	Earls Court Exhibition Hall, London, England
20 Oct	Earls Court Exhibition Hall, London, England
21 Oct	Earls Court Exhibition Hall, London, England
22 Oct	Earls Court Exhibition Hall, London, England
23 Oct	Earls Court Exhibition Hall, London, England
26 Oct	Earls Court Exhibition Hall, London, England
27 Oct	Earls Court Exhibition Hall, London, England
28 Oct	Earls Court Exhibition Hall, London, England
29 Oct	Earls Court Exhibition Hall, London, England

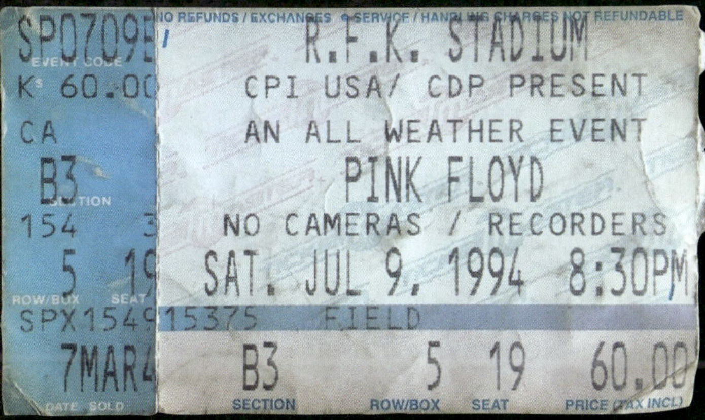

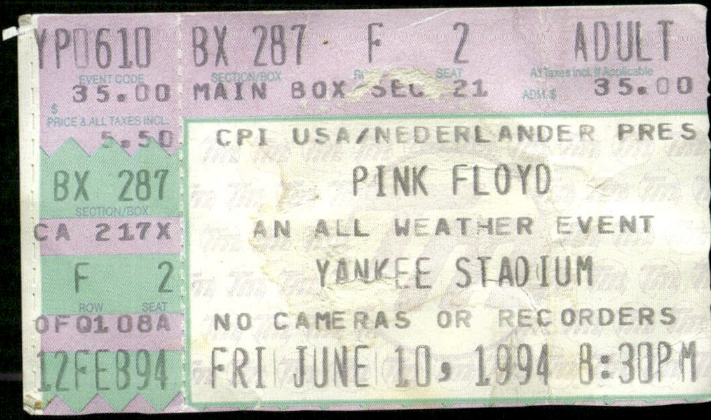

Dicesare-Engler Productions presents
PINK FLOYD
The Division Bell Tour
TUES. MAY 31, 8:30PM
at the
Pittsburgh, Three Rivers Stadium
Tickets available at all Ticket Master locations
TICKETMASTER
CHARGE BY PHONE
412-323-1919
NO REFUNDS—NO EXCHANGES
EVENT DATE AND TIME SUBJECT TO CHANGE

PINK FLOYD
EN MEXICO
9 DE ABRIL
HOT LINE
PINK FLOYD
224-1020
¡LLAMA Y ENTERATE!
nuevo foro de conciertos en el
AUTODROMO
Hermanos Rodríguez
BOLETOS DISPONIBLES EN TAQUILLAS
Venta de Boletos en el Sistema TICKETMASTER
* Taquillas del Palacio de los Deportes.
* Centros Mixup y Discolandia, Auditorio Nacional, Gimnasio Juan de la Barrera y Gran Bazar.
* Centro Telefónico al 325-9000
Con entrega a domicilio en todo el país.
OCESA

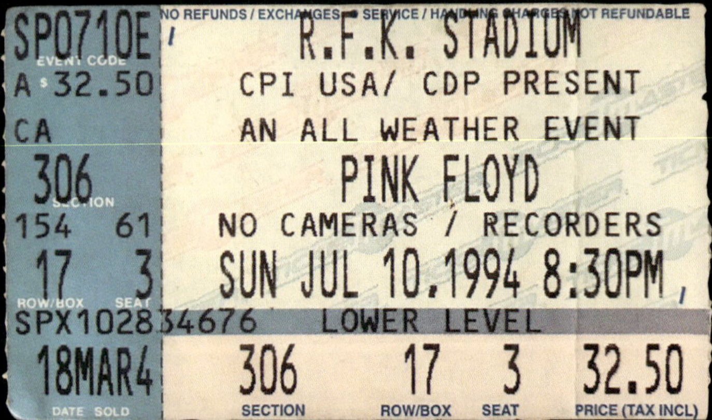
NO REFUNDS / EXCHANGES • SERVICE / HANDLING CHARGES NOT REFUNDABLE
SP0710E
EVENT CODE
A $32.50
CA
306
SECTION
154 61
17 3
ROW/BOX SEAT
SPX102834676
18MAR4
DATE SOLD
R.F.K. STADIUM
CPI USA/ CDP PRESENT
AN ALL WEATHER EVENT
PINK FLOYD
NO CAMERAS / RECORDERS
SUN JUL 10,1994 8:30PM
LOWER LEVEL
306 17 3 32.50
SECTION ROW/BOX SEAT PRICE (TAX INCL)

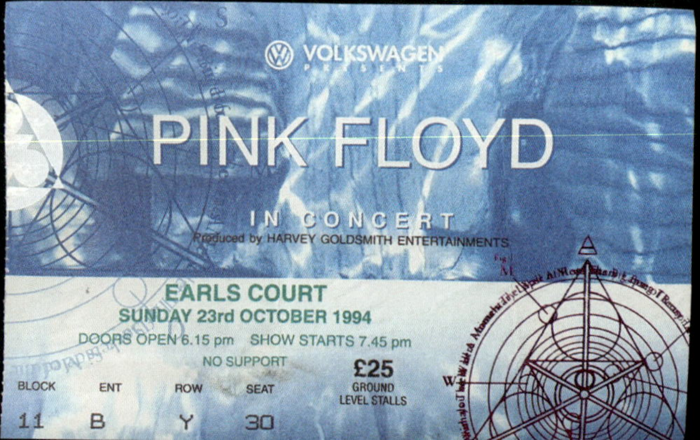
VOLKSWAGEN
PRESENTS
PINK FLOYD
IN CONCERT
Produced by HARVEY GOLDSMITH ENTERTAINMENTS
EARLS COURT
SUNDAY 23rd OCTOBER 1994
DOORS OPEN 6.15 pm SHOW STARTS 7.45 pm
NO SUPPORT
£25
GROUND LEVEL STALLS
BLOCK ENT ROW SEAT
11 B Y 30

LIVE 8 LONDON

'You can't carry on World War Three forever. If we hadn't reformed for Live 8, we'd have done it for another charity event I suspect. It's a good reason to do it – a way of building bridges for the right reasons rather than burning them down'

Nick Mason

Live 8 London – free concert. Live 8 was a string of benefit concerts that took place on July 2 2005 in the G8 states and South Africa. Timed to precede the G8 conference held at the Gleneagles Hotel in Auchterarder, Scotland from 6–8 July 2005, these events also coincided with the 20th anniversary of Live Aid.

Pink Floyd hadn't played at the original Live Aid concert in summer 1985, Roger Waters having recently officially exited the band at the time, although David Gilmour played guitar for Bryan Ferry at the event. Gilmour and Waters hadn't spoken for 20 years and their relationship was so distant in the period before Pink Floyd's celebrated reunion at Live 8, Waters had to ask organizer Bob Geldof for his former bandmate's phone number when Geldof had suggested the iconic Floyd line-up reunite for this one-off concert.

Geldof had approached Gilmour first who initially refused. No surprise there when Gilmour had once likened a reunion with Waters to *'sleeping with your ex-wife'*. But Gilmour finally conceded, saying that that Live 8 was *'bigger than those bad feelings'*, adding that, *'any squabbles Roger and the band have had in the past are so petty in this context, and if reforming for this concert will help focus attention, then it's going to be worthwhile.'*

Their first conversation in two decades was 'surprising', Gilmour admitted. As for Waters?

'Roger was immediately positive about the idea of playing together for an event that was politically in tune with his own sentiments,' said Nick Mason diplomatically, *'especially as Bob's intention was not to raise funds but to hoist a massive global rallying cry and send a clear message about needless poverty to the leaders due to attend the G8 summit at Gleneagles in Scotland.'*

Waters himself was adopting a similar 'higher-ground' stance to Gilmour and Mason.

'It's great to be asked to help Bob raise public awareness on the issues of third-world debt and poverty,' Waters enthused a few days before the July 2 event. *'The cynics will scoff. Screw 'em! Also, to be given the opportunity to put the band back together, even if it's only for a few numbers, is a big bonus.'*

Once Gilmour and Waters had been seen to bury the hatchet, albeit temporarily, both Nick Mason and Rick Wright were more than happy to fall in. Rehearsals before

Hyde Park July 2

2005

Pink Floyd plus Paul McCartney, U2, Madonna, Elton John, Chris Martin, the Boomtown Rats, Robbie Williams

Set List:

Speak to MeBreatheBreathe (reprise)Money

Wish You Were HereComfortably Numb

'It was such fun. We went in and did some rehearsals, and the moment we plugged in for the first rehearsal, it was like putting on an old shoe'

Roger Waters on rehearsing with Pink Floyd for Live 8.

Dave Gilmour of Pink Floyd performs on stage at "Live 8 London" in Hyde Park on July 2, 2005

the big day went surprisingly well – although there were disagreements about the set list. Gilmour steadfastly refused to play Pink Floyd's most recognisable radio hit, 'Another Brick in the Wall', saying its anti-education message was hardly appropriate for the event.

'Anyway, I don't like it much. It's all right but not part of the *great emotional oeuvre,'* Gilmour said *'The songs that Roger wanted were not the ones I thought we should do. The arrangements of the songs were not the way Roger wanted to do them. But I kind of insisted. There were times when Roger was struggling to not get bossy, and I was struggling to keep being bossy. I saw how arguments could have happened, but we aren't at each other's throats anymore. Getting rid of that acrimony has got to be a good thing. Who wants to have that fester in your mind the rest of your life?'*

Pink Floyd were restricted, like all the artists performing at Live 8, to a short, 20-minute set. So, they finally settled on four songs – 'Breathe' and 'Money' from 1973's 'Dark Side of the Moon', 'Wish You Were Here' from the 1975 album of the same name and 'Comfortably Numb' from 1979's 'The Wall'. Waters referred to Syd Barrett as he spoke from the Hyde Park stage. *'It's actually quite emotional to be standing up here with these three guys again, after all these years – standing to be counted with the rest of you,'* Waters said amid the opening strains of 'Wish You Were Here'. *'Anyway, we're doing this for the people who are not here – and particularly, of course, for Syd.'*

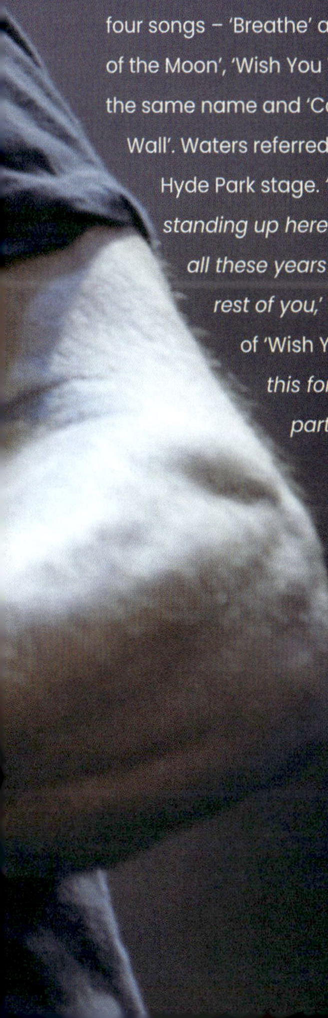

The reviews of their performance were bittersweet. So, so sweet because this iconic quartet were back together for the first time in almost 25 years but tinged with regret that they'd ever split in the first place.

'Pink Floyd had not performed together as an entire unit in over 24 years, yet their performance at Live 8 sounded like they had never stopped,' Classic Rock History eulogised. *'The band simply sounded great. David Gilmour and Roger Waters' vocals were pitch perfect and sounded just like they did on the studio recordings from 25 years earlier. Roger Waters' bass playing once again locked into those soulful defiant dark bass rhythms with his band mate and drummer Nick Mason. On keyboards, Richard Wright defined why he played such an important role in shaping the sound of Pink Floyd. And then there's David Gilmour. . . Pink Floyd fans have always known that he is simply one of rock and roll's greatest guitarists. Perhaps because of Pink Floyd's grand atmospheric progressive sound and substantial musical compositions, Gilmour's guitar playing has never gotten the credit it deserves outside of the Pink Floyd universe. Guitarists like Jeff Beck, Jimmy Page, Jimi Hendrix and Stevie Ray Vaughan have always gotten all the acclaim among lists of best classic rock guitarist. David Gilmour has always deserved to be ranked right up there with them. David Gilmour's guitar solo in "Comfortably Numb," serves simply as the best argument why Gilmour is one of the best. Like the old blues saying 'less is more', Gilmour's solo proved how meaningful that saying is. You could see how his band mates tried absorbing every second of Gilmour's solo. You can hear it in the rhythmic playing they provided underneath his solo, guiding him along the way*

and creating a pulse that helped fuel Gilmour's phrasing. In that moment, the definition of the meaning of the word "band" is defined. Any great guitarists will always state the importance of the groove that a band provides in anchoring the heart of a solo. What was most telling about Pink Floyd's Live 8 performance was the reaction of Roger Waters. During Gilmour's vocals, Roger Waters sang along joyously. He seemed to be really enjoying playing with Pink Floyd again. Watching Roger Waters, and listening to how great the band sounded simply just ignited the question, "Why? Why did this band break up?" We know there are many reasons, but the performance simply proved they should have never called it quits. Rock music is an all-powerful medium that can provide encompassing healing agents. At the end of the performance, as Floyd began their bows, David Gilmour seemed hesitant to join in the band's embrace, centre stage. Roger Waters, noticing Gilmour's hesitation, extended his hand, signalling for Gilmour to join the group bow. As David Gilmour joined Roger Waters, Nick Mason and Richard Wright, they all hung each other's arms around their shoulders, and for the last time as a group, sadly, Pink Floyd said goodbye to the world of rock and roll.'

After Pink Floyd's performance, their back catalogue saw a stunning 1300% increase in sales. Gilmour announced that he would donate his share of the proceeds to charity. Beyond that, Gilmour said Live 8 had given his younger children an opportunity to see their semi-retired old man in a whole new

Pink Floyd taking a bow at the Live 8 concert in Hyde Park, London 02 July 2005

light. *'They now understand that I'm not just this bum who lazes around the house, cooks them supper and takes them to school,'* he said.

Inevitably there were renewed questions asked about a larger-scale reunion with Waters. Pink Floyd's core four were reportedly offered as much as $150 million for a U.S. tour.

'It's completely mad,' was Gilmour's reaction, *'and we won't do it. The idea for Live 8 was a one-off. The rehearsals convinced me it wasn't something I wanted to be doing a lot of.'*

Waters appeared amenable but ultimately turned his attention to what would become a blockbuster multi-year solo presentation of *The Wall*.

'David is completely uninterested,' Waters told the press. *'After Live 8, I could have probably gone for doing some more stuff, but he's not interested.'*

Rick Wright's death on September 15 2008 seemed to put an end to any further speculation

'I think Live 8 was probably it,' Waters was to tell the BBC. *'And Live 8 was so beautiful, and Rick obviously was still with us then. If that's the way we draw a line under Pink Floyd, so be it. I won't be unhappy about that.'*

POST PINK FLOYD LIVES

Syd Barrett

'I'm disappearing, avoiding most things'

After leaving Pink Floyd, Barrett released two albums, both in 1970, entitled 'The Madcap Laughs' and 'Barrett', respectively. David Gilmour helped Syd in the studio for the first solo album and co-produced it but it was not a harmonious experience for Gilmour.

*'It was pretty tortuous and very rushed. We had very little time, particularly with "The Madcap Laughs". Syd was very difficult, we got that very frustrated feeling – "Look, it's your f**king career, mate. Why don't you get your finger out and do something?" The guy was in trouble, and was a close friend for many years before then, so it really was the least one could do.'*

Rick Wright experienced similar difficulties when playing keyboards on 'Barrett'.

'Doing Syd's record was interesting, but extremely difficult. By then it was just trying to help Syd any way we could, rather than worrying about getting the best guitar sound. You could forget about that! It was just going into the studio and trying to get him to sing.'

Gilmour, along with 'Humble Pie' drummer Jerry Shirley, backed Barrett at his one and only live performance during this time. The gig took place on June 6 1970 at the Olympia Exhibition Hall as part of a Music and Fashion Festival. The trio performed four songs – 'Terrapin', 'Gigolo Aunt', 'Effervescing Elephant' and 'Octopus'. Poor mixing left the vocals barely audible until part-way through the last number. At the end of the fourth song, Barrett unexpectedly but politely put down his guitar and walked off the stage.

In 1972, and now dividing his time between his native Cambridge and London, Syd joined with Twink (ex 'Pink Fairies') and Jack Monck, who had formerly played with the band 'Delivery', to form 'The Last Minute Put Together Boogie Band'. They supported a couple of other local acts at small, Cambridge venues. The trio then formed the short-lived band 'Stars' whose performances contained songs from the Barrett-era Pink Floyd, 'The Madcap Laughs' and 'Barrett'. Though they were initially well received at gigs in the Dandelion coffee bar and the town's Market Square, one of their gigs at Cambridge's Corn Exchange proved disastrous. A few days after this show, Twink recalled that Barrett stopped him on the street, showed him a scathing review of the gig they had played, and Barrett quit on the spot. The last time he ever performed in public was at a night of poetry and music in Cambridge during the summer of 1973.

Barrett visited the members of Pink Floyd in 1975 during the recording sessions for their ninth album, 'Wish You Were Here'. He turned up at an Abbey Road session unannounced, and watched the band working on the final mix of 'Shine On You Crazy Diamond', the song written about him. By that time, Barrett, then 29, was overweight and had shaved off all his hair – including his eyebrows. Initially, his former bandmates did not recognise him. Barrett spent part of the session brushing his teeth. Waters asked him what he thought of the song and he commented that it *'sounds a bit old'*. He left without saying goodbye. Apart from a brief encounter between Roger Waters and Barrett in Harrods a few years later – Barrett ran outside when he saw Waters, dropping his bag-full of sweets – this was the last time any member of Pink Floyd saw him.

In 1978, Barrett returned to Cambridge full-time and moved in with his mother. He reverted back to his real name of Roger, took up painting again and also gardened. He stayed out of the limelight, became annoyed when paparazzi snapped his picture and kept to himself, interacting mostly with his sister, Rosemary. Although he was hospitalized briefly, he was never officially diagnosed with a mental illness or medicated.

In 1988, EMI Records released the album, 'Opel', which included previously unreleased music that Barrett had recorded from 1968 to 1970. In 1996, Barrett was inducted into the Rock and Roll Hall of Fame as a founding member of Pink Floyd, but he did not attend the ceremony. Additionally, a number of box sets, compilations and re-issues have been released over the years.

Barrett died of pancreatic cancer on July 7 2006, at the age of 60, in Cambridge, England. In response to the news of his death, Gilmour commented:

'We are very sad to say that Roger Keith Barrett – Syd – has passed away. Do find time to play some of Syd's songs and to remember him as the madcap genius who made us all smile with his wonderfully eccentric songs about bikes, gnomes and scarecrows. His career was painfully short, yet he touched more people than he could ever know.'

In May 2007, a tribute concert, 'Madcap's Last Laugh', was held at the Barbican Centre in London in memory of Barrett. Roger Waters performed during the first half, Gilmour, Mason and Wright during the second.

Rick Wright

'I sang 'Arnold Layne' live for the first time ever since it was written, and it was fantastic to do.'

After Floyd, Rick Wright became a regular member of David Gilmour's touring band, along with former Floyd sidemen Jon Carin, Dick Parry and Guy Pratt. In 2006 he contributed keyboards and background vocals to Gilmour's solo album, 'On An Island' and performed live in Europe and North America with Gilmour that year where, in addition to playing keyboards, he sang lead vocals on 'Arnold Layne', Pink Floyd's first single from 1967, which was subsequently released as a live single. He declined an offer to join Waters and Mason on the former's 'Dark Side of the Moon Live' tour to spend more time working on a solo project. In 2006, Wright joined Gilmour and Mason for the official screening of the 'PULSE' DVD. When asked about performing again, Wright replied he would be happy on stage anywhere.

He explained that his plan was to *'meander'* along and play live whenever Gilmour required his services.

Wright's final vocal performance took place at the Syd Barrett tribute concert at The Barbican in London on May 10 2007. Once again, he sang 'Arnold Layne'. His final live performance was as part of Gilmour's band at the premiere of Gilmour's concert DVD 'Remember That Night' in September 2007 at the Odeon Leicester Square, London. After an edited version of the film had been shown, the band took to the stage to jam.

Wright died from lung cancer at his home in London on 15 September 2008, aged 65. At the time of his death, he had been working on a new solo album, thought to comprise a series of instrumental pieces.

The surviving members of Pink Floyd paid tribute to Wright. Waters said it was *'hard to overstate the importance of his musical voice in the Pink Floyd of the 60s and 70s'*, and added that he was happy they had reunited for Live 8. Mason said Wright's contributions were underrated, and that his playing *'was the sound that knitted it all together'*, comparing his 'quiet one' status in the band to George Harrison of the Beatles. Gilmour called him *'my musical partner and my friend'*, and praised Wright's ability to blend his voice with Gilmour's, on Floyd songs such as on 'Echoes'. Gilmour reiterated that it would be wrong to continue as Pink Floyd without him.

Eight days after Wright's death, Gilmour performed 'Remember A Day', a Wright composition from Pink Floyd's second album, 'A Saucerful of Secrets' on a live broadcast of 'Later. . .with Jools Holland' on BBC 2 as a tribute to Wright. Gilmour revealed that Wright had intended to perform with him that day, but had not been well enough. Gilmour also dedicated his song 'A Boat Lies Waiting' from his 2014 album 'Rattle That Lock' in Wright's memory. The song features Wright's voice sample. The lyrics define Gilmour's sadness on his friend and bandmate's demise and Wright's love for sea.

Roger Waters

'The very early days of Pink Floyd were magical. We played small auditoriums for entranced audiences, and there was a wonderful sense of communion. We got overpowered by the weight of success and numbers — not just the money but the size of the audience. I became very disenchanted. I had to make the choice of staying on the treadmill or making the braver decision to travel a more difficult path alone'

In 1984, Waters released his first solo work, 'The Pros and Cons of Hitch Hiking' and toured the album with a new band called 'Clapton' – they also performed a selection of Floyd songs. The tour drew poor ticket sales and some performances at larger venues were cancelled. In March 1985, Waters went to North America to play smaller venues with the 'Pros and Cons' plus some Pink Floyd material. In 1986, Waters contributed songs and a score to the soundtrack of the animated film 'When The Wind Blows' based on the Raymond Briggs book of the same name. The following year, he released 'Radio K.A.O.S', a concept album based on a mute man named Billy from an impoverished Welsh mining town who has the ability to physically tune into radio waves in his head.

In November 1989, the Berlin Wall fell, and in July 1990 Waters staged one of the largest and most elaborate rock concerts in history, 'The Wall – Live in Berlin', on the vacant terrain between Potsdamer Platz and the Brandenburg Gate. Waters' star-studded musicians for the production included Joni Mitchell, Van Morrison, Cyndi Lauper, Bryan Adams, Scorpions, and Sinéad O'Connor plus an East German symphony orchestra and choir, a Soviet marching band, and a pair of helicopters from the US 7th Airborne Command and Control Squadron. Waters' iconic wall for the production was 25 metres tall and 170 metres long and built across the set. Gerald Scarfe's inflatable puppets were recreated on an enlarged scale. Many rock icons received invitations to the show, although Gilmour, Mason, and Wright did not.

Waters released his third studio album, 'Amused to Death' in 1992. It was heavily influenced by the events of the Tiananmen Square protests of 1989 and the Gulf War. Waters described the record as a *'stunning piece of work'*, ranking it alongside 'Dark Side of the Moon' and 'The Wall' as one of the best of his career.

In 1999, after a 12-year hiatus from touring and a seven-year absence from the music industry, Waters embarked on the 'In the Flesh' tour, performing both solo and Pink Floyd material. The tour was a financial success in the US. In June 2002, he completed the tour with a performance in front of 70,000 people at the Glastonbury Festival, playing 15 Pink Floyd songs and five songs from his solo catalogue. In 2004 it was announced that a production of 'The Wall' was to appear on Broadway with Waters playing a prominent role in the creative direction. Reports stated that the musical contained not only the original tracks from 'The Wall' but also songs from "Dark Side of the Moon', 'Wish You Were Here' and other Pink Floyd albums, in addition to new material.

In September 2005, Waters released 'Ca Ira' (French for 'It will be fine'), an opera in three acts translated from the late Étienne Roda-Gil's French libretto based on the historical subject of the French Revolution. Live performances of the opera took place around the world at various times from 2002-2015.

In June 2006, Waters commenced 'The Dark Side of the Moon Live' tour, a two-year, world-spanning effort that began in Europe in June and North America in September. The first half of the show featured both Pink Floyd songs and Waters' solo material, while the second half included a complete live performance of 'Dark Side of the Moon' – the first time in over three decades that Waters had performed the album. The shows ended with an encore from the third side of 'The Wall'. The staging for the tour was elaborate with laser lights, fog machines, pyrotechnics, psychedelic projections, and inflatable floating Spaceman and Pig puppets controlled by a 'handler' dressed as a butcher, plus a full 360-degree quadraphonic sound system was used. Nick Mason joined Waters for the Dark Side of the Moon set and encores on various 2006 tour dates. Waters continued touring in January 2007 visiting Australia, New Zealand, Asia, Europe, South America, and back to North America in June. He performed at California's Coachella Festival in April 2008.

In September 2010, Waters commenced 'The Wall Live' tour, an updated version of the original Pink Floyd shows, featuring a complete performance of the album. Waters told the Associated Press that the tour would likely be his last, stating, *'I'm not as young as I used to be. I'm not like B.B. King, or Muddy Waters. I'm not a great vocalist or a great instrumentalist, or whatever, but I still have the fire in my belly, and I have something to say. I have a swan song in me and I think this will probably be it.'*

It wasn't, however. There was an unexpected Gilmour-Waters reunion at a low-key charity event in summer 2010. Then, at the O2 Arena in London on May 12 2011, Gilmour and Mason appeared on stage with Waters during 'The Wall Live' tour. Gilmour performed 'Comfortably Numb' before swapping his guitar for a mandolin to play 'Outside the Wall' while Mason accompanied him on the tambourine. For the first half of 2012, 'The Wall Live' topped worldwide concert ticket sales having sold more than 1.4 million tickets globally. By 2013, 'The Wall Live' had become the highest-grossing tour by a solo artist up to that date. In July 2015, Waters headlined the Newport Folk Festival in Newport, Rhode Island and 10 months later Waters was announced as one of the headline performers at the Desert Trip music festival, performing twice in October 2016. Waters returned to North America in 2017 with his 'Us + Them' tour, performing Pink Floyd and solo material. In April 2019, Waters joined 'Nick Mason's Saucerful of Secrets' band on stage at the Beacon Theatre in New York to sing the lead vocals on 'Set the Controls for the Heart of the Sun'. At the end of decade, Waters was announced as one of the top ten highest-grossing concert acts of the previous 10 years.

However, he continues to be critical of David Gilmour and the late Rick Wright, saying as recently as 2021 that, during the Floyd's hey-day, the two had *'claimed I was tone deaf and that I didn't understand music, (They'd thought) "Oh he's just a boring, kind of teacher figure who tells us what to do, but he can't tune his own guitar." Stuff like that... They were very snotty or snipey because they felt very insignificant at that point.'*

From July 2022, Roger Waters embarks on his extensive 'This Is Not A Drill' tour across North America, which was postponed due to COVID. His website states that. . .

'This Is Not A Drill is a ground-breaking new rock and roll/ cinematic extravaganza, performed in the round, it is a stunning indictment of the corporate dystopia in which we all struggle to survive, and a call to action to LOVE, PROTECT and SHARE our precious and precarious planet home. The show includes a dozen great songs from PINK FLOYD'S GOLDEN ERA along-side several new ones, words and music, same writer, same heart, same soul, same man. Could be his last hurrah. Wow! My first farewell tour! Don't miss it. Love R.'

Nick Mason

'The first night we played the club gigs it was just like being back in 1967, and the excitement of being in a band and being onstage and having an audience was absolutely terrific'

Post Pink Floyd, self-confessed petrol-head Mason mostly absorbed himself with his fleet of classic cars. He joined Gilmour and Wright again for the encore during the former's show at the Royal Albert Hall, London, on May 31 2006. That year he also stated that Pink Floyd had not officially disbanded but with the death of Wright in 2008, the band effectively came to an end. By this time, he had become friends with Waters again and saw himself as the link between Waters and Gilmour. On May 12 2007, Mason joined Waters on stage at Earls Court to play 'Dark Side of the Moon Live' and continued to play for him at various times during live shows over the years.

In 2018, Mason formed a new band, 'Nick Mason's Saucerful of Secrets', to perform Pink Floyd's early psychedelic material. Along with Mason, the band comprises of former 'Blockheads' guitarist Lee Harris, bassist and Pink Floyd collaborator Guy Pratt, vocalist and guitarist Gary Kemp of 'Spandau Ballet' and 'Orb' keyboardist, Dom Beken. As many fans had only discovered Pink Floyd with 'The Dark Side of the Moon', Mason wanted to bring their earlier material to a wider audience. During the 'Nick Mason's Saucerful of Secrets' 2019 tour of the United States, Waters joined Mason on stage in New York City for the 18 April performance and performed 'Set the Controls for the Heart of the Sun'. Mason humorously denied Mason an opportunity to bang the gong behind his drum kit – something Mason has frequently mentioned he had always wanted to do.

'Nick Mason's Saucerful of Secrets' released a live album 'Live at the Roundhouse' in September 2020. They tour Europe from Spring 2022.

'I think that returning to something that I particularly liked about being in a band, which is the enthusiasm and the sort of camaraderie of being in a band where you're all playing music together and you have a common goal,' he said recently. *'You know, it's the early days before everyone got into musical differences or arguing about royalty rates or whatever, that extraordinary ambience of working together is a really special thing. And it's a reminder that it's actually one of the great benefits of being a musician or being in a band.'*

David Gilmour

'I absolutely don't want to go back. I don't want to go and play stadiums. I'm free to do exactly what I want to do and how I want to do it'

Throughout the post-Pink Floyd era of his career, David Gilmour has continued to perform and release new music. Released eight months after Live 8, his album *'On An Island'* was hailed by critics as *'remarkable'* with The Times saying that it was *'a sort of sun-dappled Saga-rock in contentment, tempered by an attendant awareness of mortality.'* It was the tour that supported the album that found Gilmour able to stretch out and create an amazing combination of old and new. There was almost a tacit acceptance of what most of the audience wanted to hear, and Floyd warhorses were duly brought out of the stable, while – just like the Floyd had done in the 70s – the new album, in this instance, 'On An Island', was played in its entirety in the show's first half. It was on May 29 2006, at one of three nights at the Royal Albert Hall in London that David Bowie joined Gilmour on stage to sing 'Arnold Layne', originally released in 1967 when Bowie, then David Jones, was just starting out. Bowie continued by playing the guest doctor on 'Comfortably Numb'. A film of the Royal Albert Hall shows 'Remember That Night' was released on DVD on September 2007. It was heralded with a screening and live extravaganza at the Odeon Leicester Square.

In November 2006, Gilmour was awarded the CBE by Queen Elizabeth II for services to music.

'I was a bit nervous,' he confessed soon afterwards. *'The Queen said Pink Floyd had been doing it for a very long time and I had to agree. I suspect that if she has listened to Pink Floyd, it has been one of her children or grandchildren playing it and she is more likely to be the one to say, "Turn it off!' But I do not know her taste in music.'*

In July 2010, a surprise but low-key reunion between Gilmour and Roger Waters took place at a charity concert in Oxfordshire. They performed Phil Spector's 'To Know Him Is To Love Him', which is said to have regularly been one of Floyd's sound-check warm-ups in the 1970s, followed by 'Wish You Were Here', 'Comfortably Numb' and 'Another Brick in the Wall, Part 2'. It did not lead to another Pink Floyd reunion, although Gilmour did go on to appear with Waters and Mason at a 'Wall Live' concert at the O2 Arena in London in May 2011.

In 2015, Gilmour released his fourth solo album titled, 'Rattle That Lock', and that same year toured throughout Europe and South America to promote it before travelling to North

America in 2016. In 2017, Gilmour released the live album and film, 'Live at Pompeii' from the tour. The film had a special one-night showing in select cinemas before the album was released to the public a few weeks later.

In the past two decades, Gilmour has become known for his philanthropy through the DG Foundation as much as for his musical output. His increased share in sales Pink Floyd experienced after Live 8 was donated to causes close to Gilmour, as were the proceeds of his London townhouse, which he sold for £3.6 million in 2002, and donated to 'Crisis'.

'You can't live seriously in more than one house. Everything else is just a holiday home,' he said at the time.

In June 2019, Gilmour raised US$21.5 million from the Christie's sale of more than 120 of his instruments and artifacts. He donated the proceeds to 'ClientEarth', a charity which uses the power of the law to protect the planet and its people.

Gilmour performed on February 26 2020 as one of the special guests assembled by Mick Fleetwood to celebrate the life and music of 'Fleetwood Mac' founder Peter Green at The London Palladium. Throughout 2020, Gilmour also participated in a number of live streams with his family during the COVID-19 lockdowns, in which he performed songs by both Syd Barrett and Leonard Cohen. In July 2020, Gilmour released a single 'Yes, I Have Ghosts'.

His website states that *'there are no current plans for any live dates'.*

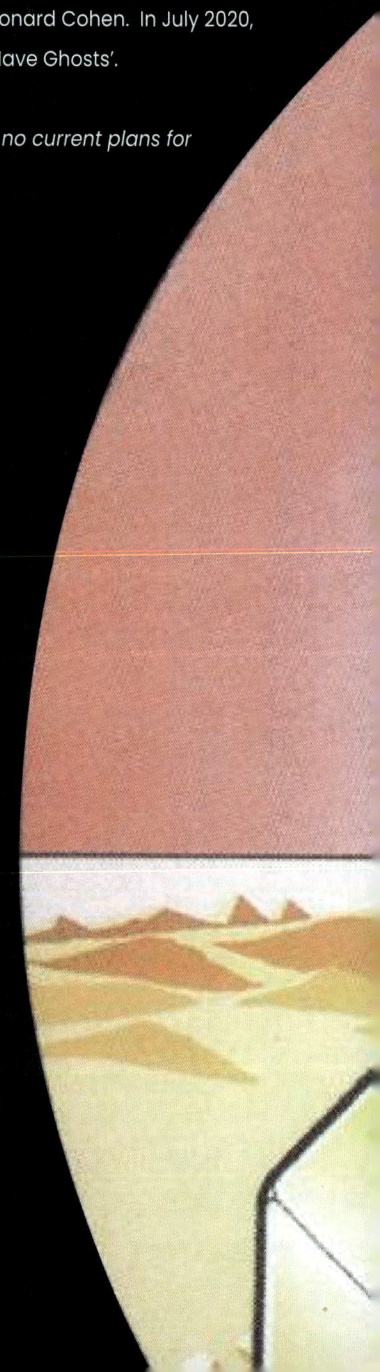

Artwork from the Wish You Were Here, Limited Edition cover

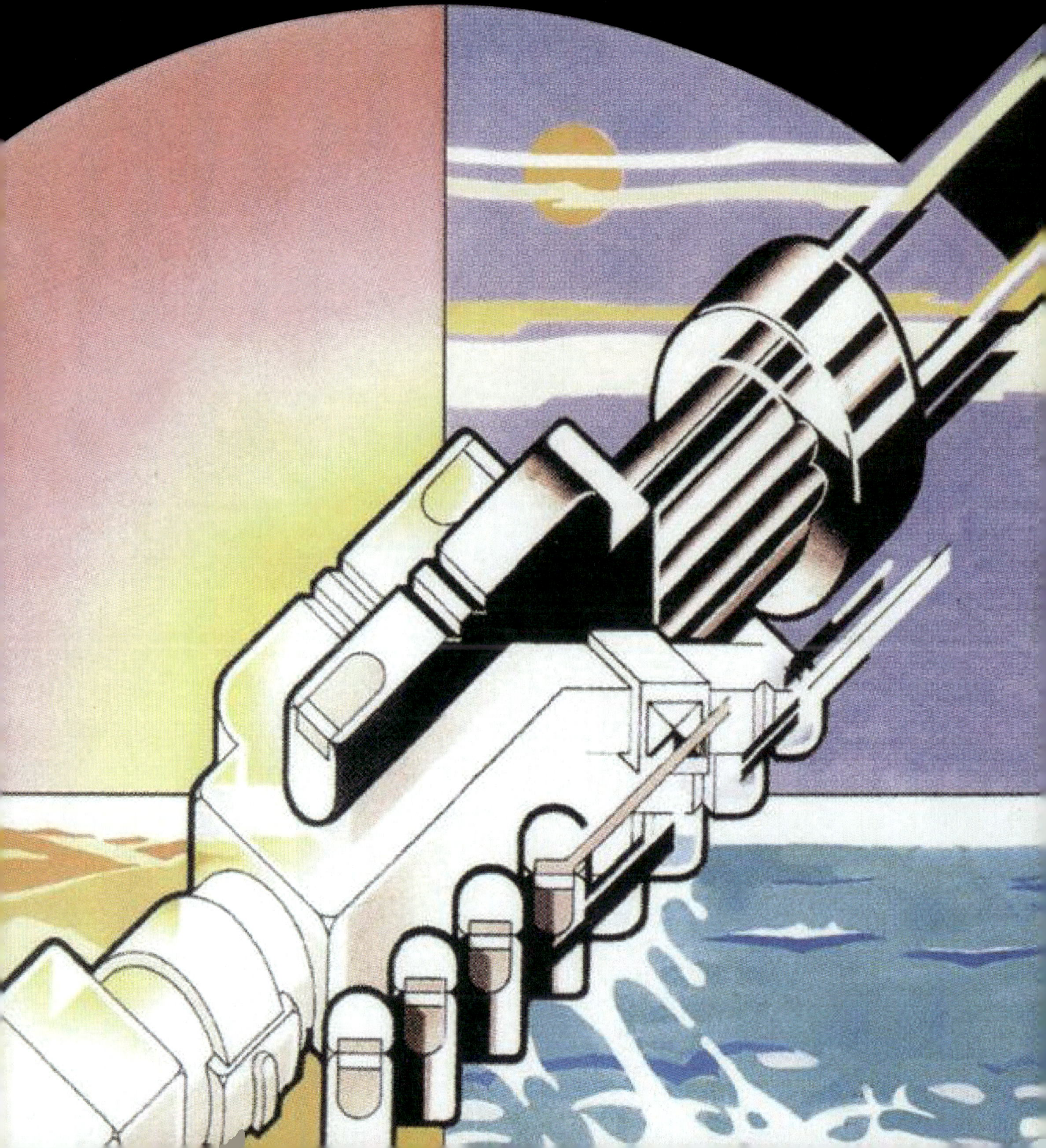

COLLABORATORS, CREATIVES & MENTORS

Pink Floyd's achievements were never solely the work of the musicians themselves. Behind every classic album and awe-inspiring tour stood producers willing to experiment, engineers capable of translating impossible ideas into reality, managers who protected the band's interests and artists who gave visual form to their imagination.

Together, these collaborators helped create a body of work that remains unique in popular music. Their contributions can be seen on every album cover, heard in every carefully crafted soundscape and felt in every unforgettable live performance. They were, in many ways, the invisible members of Pink Floyd - a creative family whose influence continues to resonate long after the final

Designer Storm Thorgerson next to his cover of the Pink Floyd album *The Dark Side of the Moon* during the opening of his exhibition 'Mind Over Matter: The Images of Pink Floyd' at the Oxo Tower Gallery in central London, 2008

UFO
ON SALE HERE
THE NEW PROJECTED SOUND-DB0241
SEE EMILY PLAY
PINK FLOYD
GAMES FOR MAY
THE PINK FLOYD

Posters for the famous UFO club from 1967, on display with other pieces in the Pink Floyd exhibition 'Their Mortal Remains' at the V&A museum in west London

Andrew King & Peter Jenner

The Men Who Opened the Door

Before Pink Floyd had a record contract, Andrew King and Peter Jenner were among the first people to recognise the band's extraordinary potential. The pair, who met as students at The London School of Economics, first encountered the group in 1966 as they became part of London's burgeoning underground music scene with regular gigs at venues such as the UFO Club. Floyd's lengthy improvisations, light shows and experimental approach made them stand out from other bands.

'They were doing something nobody else was doing,'

Jenner was to recall

Through their management company, Blackhill Enterprises, King and Jenner helped secure gigs, promoted the band to record labels and encouraged them to develop their unique identity rather than conform to commercial expectations. They stopped managing Pink Floyd in late 1968, during the turbulent period when Syd Barrett's mental health problems were forcing the band to rethink its future. They had always been particularly close to Barrett and strongly believed he could recover and continue as Pink Floyd's creative leader. When the rest of the band decided to move forward with David Gilmour as a permanent member and effectively leave Barrett behind, a split developed between King and Jenner and the band. The pair stayed on as Barrett's managers and helped launch his solo career, overseeing work that eventually resulted in the albums 'The Madcap Laughs' and 'Barrett'.

Steve O'Rourke

The Fifth Floyd

Steve O'Rourke was one of the most influential figures behind Pink Floyd's success, managing the band for more than three decades and helping transform them from a cult psychedelic act into one of the biggest-selling bands in the world. Born in 1940, O'Rourke first became involved with the music business as a promoter and manager on the London club scene. Initially working as their chauffeur and road manager, he took over management of Pink Floyd in 1968 following the departure of King and Jenner and quickly earned a reputation as a tough, practical businessman who could protect the band's interests while allowing its members considerable creative freedom. Unlike many managers of the era, O'Rourke maintained a remarkably long relationship with his clients. He guided Pink Floyd through the recording and release of landmark albums and also helped oversee the band's vast touring operations which became increasingly ambitious and technically complex during the 1970s and 80s.

O'Rourke's role became particularly important during the bitter mid-1980s dispute between Roger Waters and the other members of the band. When Waters announced he was leaving and argued that Pink Floyd should cease to exist, O'Rourke supported David Gilmour and Nick Mason in their determination to continue under the Pink Floyd name. The ensuing legal battle was eventually settled, allowing again the band to move forward. Steve O'Rourke remained Pink Floyd's manager until his death in 2003 at the age of 63.

'He was much more than a manager,' Nick Mason was quoted as saying. *'He was a friend.'*

Steve O'Rourke, the manager of Pink Floyd (wearing glasses) with the band backstage, 1974

Norman Smith

Capturing the Psychedelic Years

Norman 'Hurricane' Smith played a crucial role in Pink Floyd's early development, helping shape the sound of the band's formative recordings and bridging the gap between the British beat boom and the emerging psychedelic era. Before becoming a producer, Smith had already earned a place in music history as an engineer at Abbey Road Studios where he worked on much of The Beatles' output from 1962 to 1965. His experience in the studio made him an ideal choice when EMI signed Pink Floyd in 1967. Smith produced Pink Floyd's debut album, 'The Piper at the Gates of Dawn', recorded at Abbey Road while The Beatles were working on 'Sgt. Pepper's Lonely Hearts Club Band' in a neighbouring studio. The sessions captured Syd Barrett's whimsical songwriting and the band's experimental soundscapes with Smith helping translate their often-chaotic live performances into something that could work on record. He remained producer for the band's next albums, 'A Saucerful of Secrets', 'More' and 'Ummagumma'. As Barrett departed and David Gilmour joined, Smith found himself working with a band searching for a new identity. He encouraged the members to become more self-sufficient in the studio and supported their growing interest in longer, more ambitious compositions. By 1970, however, Pink Floyd were becoming too self-sufficient to need Smith. They wanted greater artistic control and were developing the collaborative working methods that would eventually lead to albums such as 'Meddle' and 'The Dark Side of the Moon'. There were also musical differences. Smith came from a traditional EMI and Beatles background while Pink Floyd were moving towards longer, more atmospheric and experimental pieces. Smith himself later admitted that he never entirely understood some of the band's more abstract music and was more comfortable with structured songs. After leaving Pink Floyd, Smith enjoyed chart success as a recording artist himself under the name Hurricane Smith, scoring a worldwide hit in 1971 with the song 'Don't Let It Die' and the UK No. 1 hit 'Oh Babe, What Would You Say?' in 1972.

Alan Parsons

Engineering Perfection

Alan Parsons is best known to Pink Floyd fans for his work as the engineer on the band's landmark 1973 album 'The Dark Side of the Moon', a record widely regarded as one of the greatest and best-produced albums in rock history. Born in London in 1948, Parsons joined EMI as a teenage assistant engineer and quickly established a reputation for technical innovation. Before working with Pink Floyd, he had already contributed to recordings by The Beatles, including sessions for 'Abbey Road' and 'Let It Be'. When Pink Floyd began recording 'The Dark Side of the Moon' at Abbey Road Studios in 1972, Parsons became an essential member of the creative team, helping develop many of the album's groundbreaking sonic effects. These included the seamless tape loops heard on 'Money', the atmospheric soundscapes linking songs together and the crystal-clear recording quality that became one of the album's defining characteristics. Parsons was also instrumental in recording the album's famous spoken-word snippets. He and the band interviewed studio staff, road crew members and friends, asking questions about life, madness and mortality. Their responses became woven throughout the record, adding to its conceptual depth and sense of realism. The success of 'The Dark Side of the Moon' brought Parsons international recognition, earning him a Grammy nomination and establishing him as one of Britain's leading engineers. Although he did not work on subsequent Pink Floyd albums, his influence on the sound of the album remains immense. Parsons himself was later to say that the album was

'a very special combination of musicianship and technology'.

Parsons later moved into production and recording as an artist in his own right, forming The Alan Parsons Project with songwriter Eric Woolfson in 1975. The duo enjoyed worldwide success with albums such as 'Tales of Mystery and Imagination', 'I Robot' and 'Eye in the Sky', proving that the engineer who helped shape Pink Floyd's masterpiece was also a major creative force in his own right.

James Guthrie

Guardian of the Catalogue

James Guthrie is one of the most important figures in Pink Floyd's later career, renowned for his meticulous approach to sound and also his long-standing role as the custodian of the band's recorded legacy. Born in England and raised partly in Canada, Guthrie began his career as a recording engineer before attracting attention for his work with artists including The Bay City Rollers and Runner. In 1978, at just 24 years old, he was chosen by Roger Waters and the band to produce 'The Wall', succeeding a line of distinguished producers and engineers who had helped shape Pink Floyd's sound. The recording of 'The Wall' was an immense undertaking involving multiple studios, complex arrangements and increasing tensions within the band. Guthrie's calm, highly organised working style proved invaluable. He helped turn Roger Waters' ambitious concept into a coherent double album, balancing its theatrical storytelling with the sonic depth and polish for which Pink Floyd had become famous. His contribution can be heard throughout the record, from the stark intimacy of 'Nobody Home' to the epic scale of 'Comfortably Numb' - widely regarded as one of the band's finest recordings.

Perhaps his greatest contribution has come in the decades since Pink Floyd's commercial peak. Since the 1980s, Guthrie has overseen many of the band's remastering, remixing and archival projects, becoming the trusted guardian of their catalogue. He was responsible for acclaimed remasters of albums including 'The Dark Side of the Moon', 'Wish You Were Here' and 'The Wall'.

Guthrie is regarded as one of the finest engineers of his generation. His obsession with detail, clarity and faithful reproduction of the original recordings has helped preserve Pink Floyd's music for new audiences, making him not just a producer but the band's principal sonic archivist. Today, few people are more closely associated with the sound quality and preservation of Pink Floyd's recorded legacy.

Bob Ezrin

The Architect of The Wall

Bob Ezrin was one of the key creative forces behind some of Pink Floyd's most ambitious and theatrical work, bringing a fresh perspective that helped the band reach new artistic and commercial heights. Born in Toronto, Canada in 1949, Ezrin had already established himself as one of rock's most innovative producers before joining forces with Pink Floyd. He had worked extensively with Alice Cooper, producing classic albums such as 'School's Out' and 'Billion Dollar Babies' and had developed a reputation for transforming ambitious ideas into compelling, accessible records.

Ezrin became involved with Pink Floyd in 1978 when Roger Waters presented his concept for 'The Wall'. Recognising the project's potential, Ezrin helped shape Waters' sprawling narrative into a more focused and dramatic work. He is often credited with acting as a bridge between Waters' conceptual vision and the practical realities of making a commercially viable album. His contributions included refining the storyline, restructuring parts of the album and encouraging stronger emotional and musical dynamics throughout. One of Ezrin's most significant achievements was helping develop the album's cinematic quality. Drawing on his experience with theatrical rock productions, he encouraged arrangements that heightened the drama and broadened the record's appeal. He also played a major role in the creation of the album's biggest hit, 'Another Brick in the Wall (Part 2)'. It was reportedly Ezrin who suggested adding the now-famous children's choir and a disco-influenced groove, helping transform the track into Pink Floyd's only UK and US Number One single. Ezrin later co-produced 'A Momentary Lapse of Reason', working closely with David Gilmour after Roger Waters' departure. His involvement helped steer Pink Floyd into a new era and re-establish the band as a major touring and recording act.

Beyond Pink Floyd, Ezrin's career has encompassed an extraordinary range of artists, including Lou Reed, Peter Gabriel, Kiss, Rod Stewart, Taylor Swift and Deep Purple. Widely respected for his ability to combine artistic ambition with mainstream appeal, he remains one of the most influential producers in modern rock history.

Hipgnosis

Creating the Visual Language of Pink Floyd

Hipgnosis was the visionary design collective responsible for many of Pink Floyd's most iconic album covers, creating images that became almost as famous as the music itself. Founded in London in 1968 by designers Storm Thorgerson and Aubrey Powell - and joined several years later by Peter Christopherson - Hipgnosis revolutionised album artwork by treating record sleeves as works of art rather than mere packaging. Their relationship with Pink Floyd began through personal connections - Thorgerson had attended school with Syd Barrett and Roger Waters. This trust gave Hipgnosis an unusual degree of creative freedom, allowing them to develop striking, often surreal imagery that perfectly complemented the band's music.

'We just sit in a very ordinary room, listen to Floyd music, and talk,' Thorgerson once commented about the collaboration.

Among their most celebrated Floyd creations are the prism and spectrum of 'The Dark Side of the Moon', the burning businessman shaking hands at a power station on 'Wish You Were Here', the pig floating above Battersea Power Station on 'Animals' and the faceless figures embracing beneath the sea on 'Meddle'. Long before the advent of digital manipulation, these images were achieved largely through photography and practical effects.

Storm Thorgerson was particularly known for his refusal to use obvious visual interpretations of song lyrics. Instead, he sought to create images that evoked the mood,

themes and emotional resonance of the music. The cover of 'The Dark Side of the Moon', designed with illustrator George Hardie, is perhaps the ultimate example - simple, elegant and instantly recognisable worldwide.

Hipgnosis also worked with numerous major artists including Led Zeppelin, Genesis, Paul McCartney, Peter Gabriel and 10cc. However, their collaboration with Pink Floyd remains their defining achievement.

Aubrey Powell, of art design group Hipgnosis, with art for Pink Floyd's *Wish You Were Here*, 2022

Gerald Scarfe is one of the most important visual artists associated with Pink Floyd - best known for creating the disturbing, unforgettable imagery that defined 'The Wall' and its subsequent stage show and film adaptation. Born in London in 1936, Scarfe first gained prominence as a political cartoonist, working for publications including The Sunday Times. His drawing style was instantly recognisable - grotesque, exaggerated and often darkly satirical. His caricatures of politicians and public figures won acclaim for their sharp wit and emotional intensity, qualities that would later make him a perfect collaborator for Roger Waters.

'Roger gave me complete freedom to visualise his ideas,'

Scarfe later remarked.

He became involved with Pink Floyd in 1979 when Waters sought an artist capable of bringing 'The Wall's' themes of alienation, authoritarianism and psychological collapse to life. The result was a series of haunting characters that have become inseparable from the album itself. These included the monstrous schoolmaster, the domineering mother, the grotesque wife, the marching hammers and the terrifying judge that appears during Pink's surreal trial sequence. His illustrations extended far beyond the album sleeve. For Pink Floyd's spectacular 'The Wall' concerts of 1980–81, Scarfe created enormous, animated projections that were shown across the giant wall constructed on stage. The animations added a theatrical and cinematic dimension to the performances, transforming them into one of the most ambitious live productions in rock history. Scarfe's work reached an even wider audience with the film 'Pink Floyd – The Wall' directed by Alan Parker and starring Bob Geldof. The film's animated sequences, based on Scarfe's original artwork, remain among the most striking and unsettling images ever created for a music-related project. The marching hammers, in particular, have become one of the most enduring visual symbols in rock culture.

Gerald Scarfe's creations brought to life in Pink Floyd's 'The Wall' exhibit at the Rock and Roll Hall of Fame

16

Mark Fisher

Master of the Spectacle

Mark Fisher was the man who transformed Pink Floyd's concerts from rock shows into architectural spectacles - helping define the visual grandeur that became a hallmark of the band's legacy. Trained as an architect, he brought a designer's eye and engineer's precision to live performance, creating structures that were as important to the audience experience as the music itself. His association with Pink Floyd began in the mid-1970s and reached full expression on the 1977 'In the Flesh' tour, where he helped develop the band's innovative stage environments. His greatest achievement came with 'The Wall' concerts of 1980–81 when he worked alongside Roger Waters and Gerald Scarfe to create the enormous wall that was gradually built across the stage during the performance. The production was unlike anything audiences had ever seen and remains one of the most ambitious live shows in rock history. Fisher also designed the spectacular staging for Roger Waters' 1990 Berlin performance of 'The Wall' where a 170-metre-long wall was erected on the former no-man's-land between East and West Berlin in front of hundreds of thousands of spectators. He later returned to work on Pink Floyd's 1994 'The Division Bell' tour, creating one of the most technologically advanced stage productions of its era. Outside Pink Floyd, Fisher became the world's most celebrated concert designer, creating landmark tours for U2, The Rolling Stones, Tina Turner and Madonna, as well as contributing to the opening ceremonies of the Beijing 2008 Olympic Games and the London 2012 Olympic Games.

Rotating flower-petal mirror ball designed by Mark Fisher, used to reflect spotlights during Pink Floyd concerts from 1975 to 1977

Clare Torry

The Voice That Defined an Album

A London-born session singer and songwriter, Torry was a regular at Abbey Road Studios during the late 1960s and early 1970s. When Pink Floyd were struggling to complete a piece known as 'The Great Gig in the Sky', engineer Alan Parsons suggested Torry with whom he had previously worked. She arrived at Abbey Road on 21 January 1973 and was given only the vaguest instructions - rather than sing lyrics, she was asked to express emotions about life, death and fear using her voice alone. The result was one of the most celebrated vocal performances in rock history.

Torry improvised the soaring, wordless vocal almost entirely on the spot, recording a handful of takes from which the final performance was assembled. Ironically, she left the session believing she had not done particularly well – *'I thought I'd ruined it'* - while those in the control room were astonished by what they had heard. She was paid the standard session fee of £30 for her work. For many years, Torry's contribution was acknowledged only as a performance. However, in 2004 she successfully pursued a claim that her improvised vocal amounted to a compositional contribution. A settlement was reached in 2005, after which all releases of 'The Dark Side of the Moon' credited 'The Great Gig in the Sky' to both Richard Wright and Clare Torry. Beyond Pink Floyd, Torry enjoyed a successful career as a session vocalist, working with artists including Olivia Newton-John, Culture Club, Meat Loaf and The Alan Parsons Project. Yet her legacy will always be tied to those unforgettable four minutes on 'The Great Gig in the Sky'.

STUDIO ALBUM BY ALBUM

The Piper At The Gates of Dawn (1967)

The Dawn of a Different Kind of Psychedelia

ALBUM	RECORDED	LABEL (UK ORIGINAL)	PRODUCER(S)	RECORDING LOCATION(S)	UK PEAK	US PEAK
The Piper at the Gates of Dawn	Feb-Jun 1967	Columbia	Norman Smith	Abbey Road Studios, London	#6	#131

Track *Songwriter(s)*

Side One

1. **Astronomy Domine** *Syd Barrett*
2. **Lucifer Sam** *Syd Barrett*
3. **Matilda Mother** *Syd Barrett*
4. **Flaming** *Syd Barrett*
5. **Pow R. Toc H.** *Syd Barrett, Roger Waters, Richard Wright, Nick Mason*
6. **Take Up Thy Stethoscope and Walk** *Roger Waters*

Side Two

1. **Interstellar Overdrive** *Syd Barrett, Roger Waters, Richard Wright, Nick Mason*
2. **The Gnome** *Syd Barrett*
3. **Chapter 24** *Syd Barrett*
4. **The Scarecrow** *Syd Barrett*
5. **Bike** *Syd Barrett*

Released on 4 August 1967, 'The Piper at the Gates of Dawn' remains one of the most ground-breaking debut albums in rock history. While much of that so-called Summer of Love was drenched in Californian optimism, Pink Floyd emerged from London's underground with something stranger, darker and infinitely more imaginative. This was psychedelia viewed through a playful, whimsical, unsettling and utterly original kaleidoscope. At the heart of the album was Syd Barrett, Pink Floyd's founding visionary. With his tousled curls, impish smile and seemingly limitless imagination, Barrett wrote or co-wrote most of the record and shaped its unique character. Drawing inspiration from children's literature, science fiction, fairy tales and the emerging counterculture, he created songs that felt less like conventional pop and more like journeys into parallel worlds.

Recorded at EMI's Abbey Road Studios between February and May 1967, the album was made in the very building where The Beatles were simultaneously crafting 'Sgt. Pepper's Lonely Hearts Club Band'. Yet while both bands were exploring new frontiers, Pink Floyd's approach was distinctly their own. Roger Waters, Richard Wright and Nick Mason provided a platform for Barrett's imagination, creating swirling soundscapes filled with echoing guitars, inventive keyboard textures and experimental studio effects.

The opening track 'Astronomy Domine' announced that this was no ordinary rock album. A cosmic voyage through the solar system, it combined space-age imagery with an exhilarating sense of adventure. Elsewhere, songs such as 'Lucifer Sam', 'The Gnome' and 'Scarecrow' revealed Barrett's fascination with eccentric characters and dreamlike storytelling.

'Syd was the guiding light of the early band. He was extraordinarily imaginative,'

David Gilmour was to later reflect.

The album's centrepiece remains 'Interstellar Overdrive', a sprawling instrumental that captured the improvisational spirit of Pink Floyd's legendary live performances at London's UFO Club. Wild, unpredictable and years ahead of its time, the track helped lay the foundations for progressive rock while also influencing generations of experimental musicians. Yet beneath the whimsy lay hints of the fragility that would soon engulf Barrett. His songwriting possessed an innocence that could suddenly turn unsettling. In retrospect, the album offers a glimpse into the extraordinary creativity that made Barrett a cult hero but also the vulnerability that would eventually lead to his breakdown and departure from the band.

Critics and audiences initially struggled to know quite what to make of Pink Floyd. The album reached No.6 in the UK charts, but its true significance emerged over time. Today, 'The Piper at the Gates of Dawn' is widely regarded as one of the defining records of the psychedelic era and one of the most influential British debut albums ever recorded.

For Pink Floyd, it was the beginning of a remarkable journey. For Syd Barrett, it was both a triumph and the start of a tragedy. For listeners, it remains a magical portal into a world where bicycles gleam, scarecrows sing and the stars themselves seem within reach.

A Saucerful of Secrets (1968)

Farewell to a Visionary

ALBUM	RECORDED	LABEL (UK ORIGINAL)	PRODUCER(S)	RECORDING LOCATION(S)	UK PEAK	US PEAK
A Saucerful of Secrets	Aug 1967 - Apr 1968	Columbia	Norman Smith	Abbey Road Studios, London	#9	#58

Track *Songwriter(s)*

Side One

1. Let There Be More Light *Roger Waters*
2. Remember a Day *Richard Wright*
3. Set the Controls for the Heart of the Sun *Roger Waters*
4. Corporal Clegg *Roger Waters*

Side Two

1. A Saucerful of Secrets *David Gilmour, Roger Waters, Richard Wright, Nick Mason*
2. See-Saw *Richard Wright*
3. Jugband Blues *Syd Barrett*

If 'The Piper at the Gates of Dawn' captured Pink Floyd at their most innocent and imaginative, 'A Saucerful of Secrets' documented a band in the midst of profound change. Released on 29 June 1968, it stands as both the final chapter of the Syd Barrett era and the first glimpse of the Pink Floyd that would conquer the world.

The circumstances surrounding the album were far from ideal. Barrett's behaviour had become increasingly erratic, making recording sessions unpredictable. While he still contributed to the album, his role was diminishing rapidly. The arrival of David Gilmour in early 1968 provided much-needed stability, initially as a fifth member intended to support Barrett before eventually replacing him altogether. As a result, 'A Saucerful of Secrets' feels fragmented but wonderfully so. Several tracks still bear Barrett's unmistakable fingerprints. The haunting 'Jugband Blues', his final composition for the group, is one of the most poignant farewells in rock history. Its cryptic lyrics and melancholy tone seem to acknowledge his growing disconnection from both the band and reality itself. Elsewhere, the remaining members began developing new musical directions. Roger Waters emerged as an increasingly confident songwriter while Richard Wright contributed some of the album's most memorable moments, including the ethereal 'Remember a Day'. Nick Mason's drumming became more adventurous while Gilmour's guitar work added a new level of precision and emotional depth. The title track represented the future. Lasting almost twelve minutes, 'A Saucerful of Secrets' abandoned conventional song structures in favour of an ambitious instrumental journey. Moving from chaos to serenity, it demonstrated the band's growing fascination with atmosphere, dynamics and storytelling through sound. These ideas would later form the foundations of their most celebrated work.

Visually, the album also marked a milestone. It featured the first cover designed by the collective that would become known as Hipgnosis, beginning one of the most important artist-designer relationships in music history. Although it lacked the commercial impact of later albums, 'A Saucerful of Secrets' reached No. 9 in the UK charts and established that Pink Floyd could survive beyond Barrett. As Roger Waters remarked,

'Syd was a genius but the band had to move on.'

'A Saucerful of Secrets' proved that the remaining members possessed enough creativity and ambition to forge a new identity. The album remains fascinating because it captures a band suspended between two worlds - the psychedelic whimsy of the past and the expansive progressive rock future that lay ahead. It is the sound of transition, uncertainty and resilience.

More (1969)

Pink Floyd Goes to the Movies

ALBUM	RECORDED	LABEL (UK ORIGINAL)	PRODUCER(S)	RECORDING LOCATION(S)	UK PEAK	US PEAK
More	Jan-Feb 1969	Columbia / Harvest	Pink Floyd	Pye Studios, London	#9	#153

Track *Songwriter(s)*

Side One

1. Cirrus Minor *Roger Waters*
2. The Nile Song *Roger Waters*
3. Crying Song *Roger Waters*
4. Up the Khyber *David Gilmour, Roger Waters*
5. Green Is the Colour *Roger Waters*
6. Cymbaline *Roger Waters*
7. Party Sequence *Pink Floyd*

Side Two

1. Main Theme *Pink Floyd*
2. Ibiza Bar *Roger Waters, Richard Wright, David Gilmour, Nick Mason*
3. More Blues *Pink Floyd*
4. Quicksilver *Pink Floyd*
5. A Spanish Piece *David Gilmour*
6. Dramatic Theme *Pink Floyd*

By 1969, Pink Floyd had survived the departure of Syd Barrett and begun to establish themselves as one of Britain's most adventurous live acts. Yet few could have predicted that their next project would be a film soundtrack. Released on 27 July 1969, 'More' revealed another side of the band and marked the beginning of a long relationship with cinema. The album was written for French director Barbet Schroeder's film of the same name - a story of young lovers whose lives are consumed by heroin addiction on the island of Ibiza. Unlike the sprawling experimental pieces that had become a staple of Floyd's concerts, the soundtrack demanded concise songs tailored to specific scenes and moods.

The result was one of the most varied albums in the band's catalogue. Gentle acoustic pieces sit alongside heavy rock workouts, pastoral ballads and atmospheric instrumentals. It is a record that refuses to settle into a single identity, reflecting both the demands of the film and the band's willingness to explore new territory. Tracks such as 'Green Is the Colour' and 'Cymbaline' showcased a growing sophistication in Roger Waters' songwriting. The former possess a delicate beauty while the latter hints at the themes of anxiety and alienation that would become

central to later albums. At the opposite end of the spectrum sits 'The Nile Song' – one of the heaviest recordings Pink Floyd ever made which foreshadowed elements of hard rock and heavy metal. David Gilmour's contribution became increasingly significant throughout the sessions – his melodic instincts and distinctive guitar tone helping to shape the band's evolving sound while Richard Wright's keyboards added colour and atmosphere.

Though often overlooked in comparison with the albums that followed, 'More' played a crucial role in Pink Floyd's development. The experience taught them how to use music to support narrative and emotion, skills they would later employ to extraordinary effect on concept albums such as 'The Dark Side of the Moon' and 'The Wall'.

'We were learning how music could tell a story without words,' commented David Gilmour.

The album reached No. 9 in the UK and strengthened the band's reputation as musical explorers. More than half a century later, it remains an intriguing snapshot of Pink Floyd at a crossroads – experimenting with styles, refining their craft and searching for a new direction.

Ummagumma (1969)

Experimentation Without Limits

Track *Songwriter(s)*

Side One (Live)
1. **Astronomy Domine** *Syd Barrett*
2. **Careful with That Axe, Eugene** *Roger Waters, Richard Wright, David Gilmour, Nick Mason*

Side Two (Live)
1. **Set the Controls for the Heart of the Sun** *Roger Waters*
2. **A Saucerful of Secrets** *David Gilmour, Roger Waters, Richard Wright, Nick Mason*

Side Three (Studio)
1. **Sysyphus Part 1** *Richard Wright*
2. **Sysyphus Part 2** *Richard Wright*
3. **Sysyphus Part 3** *Richard Wright*
4. **Sysyphus Part 4** *Richard Wright*
5. **Grantchester Meadows** *Roger Waters*
6. **Several Species of Small Furry Animals Gathered Together in a Cave and Grooving with a Pict** *Roger Waters*

Side Four (Studio)
1. **The Narrow Way Part 1** *David Gilmour*
2. **The Narrow Way Part 2** *David Gilmour*
3. **The Narrow Way Part 3** *David Gilmour*
4. **The Grand Vizier's Garden Party Part 1 – Entrance** *Nick Mason*
5. **The Grand Vizier's Garden Party Part 2 – Entertainment** *Nick Mason*
6. **The Grand Vizier's Garden Party Part 3 – Exit** *Nick Mason*

Released in November 1969, 'Ummagumma' remains one of the strangest and most divisive albums in Pink Floyd's catalogue. The original double album consisted of two live sides and two studio sides. Truly experimental, it captured a band determined to push beyond conventional rock music and test the limits of their creativity.

The live recordings, taken from performances in Birmingham and Manchester, showcased Pink Floyd's reputation as one of the most adventurous acts on the concert circuit. Extended versions of 'Astronomy Domine', 'Set the Controls for the Heart of the Sun', 'Careful with That Axe, Eugene' demonstrated their ability to transform songs into immersive sonic experiences. The studio portion was even more ambitious. Each member was given complete freedom to create and oversee his own compositions. Roger Waters contributed the pastoral suite 'Grantchester Meadows' and the unsettling 'Several Species of Small Furry Animals Gathered Together in a Cave and Grooving with a Pict'. Richard Wright explored avant-garde classical influences on 'Sysyphus' while Nick Mason delivered the eccentric 'The Grand Vizier's Garden Party'. David Gilmour offered the atmospheric 'The Narrow Way' - hinting at the melodic strengths that would later define his work.

'We were just trying everything we could think of,' said Nick Mason.

ALBUM	RECORDED	LABEL (UK ORIGINAL)	PRODUCER(S)	RECORDING LOCATION(S)	UK PEAK	US PEAK
Ummagumma	Apr-Jun 1969 (studio), live Apr-May 1969	Harvest	Pink Floyd	EMI Studios, London; Mothers Club Birmingham; Manchester College of Commerce	#5	#74

Not every experiment succeeded. Even the band later admitted that some ideas were more interesting in theory than execution. Yet that willingness to take risks became one of Pink Floyd's defining characteristics. Commercially, the album performed strongly, reaching No. 5 in the UK and proving that audiences were willing to follow the band into increasingly unconventional territory. More importantly, it encouraged the members to think on a larger scale thus setting the stage for the ambitious works of the 1970s.

Today, 'Ummagumma' stands as a fascinating document of artistic freedom. Not always an easy listen, it offers a rare glimpse into four musicians exploring their individual identities before combining their talents to create some of rock's greatest masterpieces.

Atom Heart Mother (1970)

Thinking Bigger Than Ever Before

ALBUM	RECORDED	LABEL (UK ORIGINAL)	PRODUCER(S)	RECORDING LOCATION(S)	UK PEAK	US PEAK
Atom Heart Mother	Mar-Aug 1970	Pink Floyd & Ron Geesin	Norman Smith	Abbey Road Studios, London	#1	#55

Track *Songwriter(s)*

Side One

1. **Atom Heart Mother** *David Gilmour, Roger Waters, Richard Wright, Nick Mason, Ron Geesin*

Side Two

1. **If** *Roger Waters*
2. **Summer '68** *Richard Wright*
3. **Fat Old Sun** *David Gilmour*
4. **Alan's Psychedelic Breakfast** *David Gilmour, Roger Waters, Richard Wright, Nick Mason*

By 1970, Pink Floyd had spent several years experimenting with sound, structure and performance. With 'Atom Heart Mother', released on 2 October 1970, they took their most ambitious leap yet. This was the album where the band began to think on a grand scale, blending rock music with orchestral arrangements and proving they could create works that stretched far beyond the boundaries of conventional pop. The centrepiece was the 23-minute title suite, a sprawling composition developed collaboratively by the four band members with orchestral arrangements by avant-garde composer Ron Geesin. Divided into six sections, it moved between thunderous brass passages, delicate choral interludes and atmospheric instrumental moments. Nothing quite like it had appeared in mainstream rock before.

The album's famously surreal cover – a simple photograph of a cow standing in a field with no band name or album title – reflected Pink Floyd's growing confidence. While most groups relied on elaborate artwork and branding, Pink Floyd chose complete ambiguity. It was a statement that the music should speak for itself. The second half of the album revealed a softer, more pastoral side. Waters' 'If' offered an unusually personal glimpse into his inner thoughts while Wright's 'Summer '68' reflected on life on the road. Gilmour's beautiful folk-inspired 'Fat Old Sun' became a concert favourite, showcasing his growing confidence as both songwriter and vocalist.

Commercially the gamble paid off. 'Atom Heart Mother' became Pink Floyd's first UK No.1, confirming their rise from cult favourites to major recording artists. Although several band members later expressed mixed feelings about the title suite – opined David Gilmour some years later - the album remains a crucial stepping stone between the experimentation of the late 1960s and the masterpieces that would follow.

*'Atom Heart Mother was a good idea but it was dreadful... it's s**t - possibly our lowest point artistically'*

Meddle (1971)

The Sound of Pink Floyd Emerging

ALBUM	RECORDED	LABEL (UK ORIGINAL)	PRODUCER(S)	RECORDING LOCATION(S)	UK PEAK	US PEAK
Meddle	Jan-Aug 1971	Harvest	Pink Floyd	AIR Studios, Abbey Road Studios, Morgan Studios	#3	#70

If one album can be described as the moment Pink Floyd truly found themselves, it is 'Meddle'. Released on 5 November 1971, the record bridged the gap between the experimental years and the classic era that would soon make the band one of the biggest names in music. The album was created through an unusually collaborative process. Rather than arriving with fully formed songs, the band spent months developing ideas in rehearsal rooms and studios. While some experiments went nowhere, others became the foundation of one of the most important albums in their history.

Track *Songwriter(s)*

Side One

1. **One of These Days** *David Gilmour, Roger Waters, Richard Wright, Nick Mason*
2. **A Pillow of Winds** *David Gilmour, Roger Waters*
3. **Fearless** *David Gilmour, Roger Waters*
4. **San Tropez** *Roger Waters*
5. **Seamus** *David Gilmour, Roger Waters, Richard Wright, Nick Mason*

Side Two

1. **Echoes** *David Gilmour, Roger Waters, Richard Wright, Nick Mason*

The opening track - 'One of These Days' - remains one of the most thrilling recordings in the Floyd catalogue. Driven by Nick Mason's ominous spoken line – *'One of these days I'm going to cut you into little pieces'* - and propelled by a hypnotic bass riff, it demonstrated the band's ability to create tension and drama with remarkable economy. Elsewhere, 'Fearless' offered a more reflective mood, combining Gilmour's warm vocals with a memorable football crowd recording from Liverpool's Kop. Tracks such as 'San Tropez' and 'A Pillow of Winds' revealed a newfound confidence in melody and songwriting. Yet everything on the album ultimately points towards its extraordinary closing piece, 'Echoes'. Lasting more than 23 minutes, the track occupies the entire second side of the original LP and remains one of Pink Floyd's greatest achievements. Beginning with Wright's now-famous 'ping' note,

The inner sleeve contains the last to show a group photo of this lineup of Pink Floyd. (L-R): Roger Waters, Nick Mason, David Gilmour, Richard Wright

'Echoes' unfolds as a journey through mystery, beauty and chaos before emerging into radiant resolution. The song's themes of communication, connection and shared humanity would later reappear in 'The Dark Side of the Moon' and 'The Division Bell'.

'It was the first time we realised we could tackle something genuinely epic,' remarked David Gilmour.

Critics immediately recognised that Pink Floyd had created something special. While previous albums often felt exploratory, 'Meddle' possessed a sense of purpose and cohesion. It was the sound of four musicians learning how to combine experimentation with accessibility. Without 'Meddle', there would almost certainly be no 'The Dark Side of the Moon'.

Obscured by Clouds (1972)

The Forgotten Gem

ALBUM	RECORDED	LABEL (UK ORIGINAL)	PRODUCER(S)	RECORDING LOCATION(S)	UK PEAK	US PEAK
Obscured by Clouds	Feb-Mar 1972	Harvest	Pink Floyd	Château d'Hérouville, France	#6	#46

Track *Songwriter(s)*

Side One

1. **Obscured by Clouds** *David Gilmour, Roger Waters*
2. **When You're In** *David Gilmour, Roger Waters, Richard Wright, Nick Mason*
3. **Burning Bridges** *Roger Waters, Richard Wright*
4. **The Gold It's in the...** *Roger Waters*
5. **Wot's... Uh the Deal** *David Gilmour, Roger Waters*
6. **Mudmen** *David Gilmour, Richard Wright*

Side Two

1. **Childhood's End** *David Gilmour*
2. **Free Four** *Roger Waters,*
3. **Stay** *Roger Waters, Richard Wright*
4. **Absolutely Curtains** *David Gilmour, Roger Waters, Richard Wright, Nick Mason*

Overshadowed by the monumental success of the albums that followed, 'Obscured by Clouds' is often described as Pink Floyd's most underrated record. Released on 2 June 1972, it arrived just months before the band began recording 'The Dark Side of the Moon' and offers a fascinating glimpse of a group on the brink of greatness. Written as the soundtrack for Barbet Schroeder's film 'La Vallée', it was recorded quickly between touring commitments. Unlike many previous projects the band worked with unusual speed and spontaneity and created an album that feels refreshingly direct. In addition, the recording process itself was stress-free.

'It was one of the easiest albums we ever made,' David Gilmour was to reflect.

The record balances atmospheric instrumentals with some of the strongest conventional songs Pink Floyd had yet produced. 'Free Four' saw Waters reflect on mortality with a surprisingly upbeat melody while 'Childhood's End' featured one of Gilmour's finest early compositions. Tracks such as 'Wot's... Uh the Deal' and 'Stay' demonstrated the growing maturity of the band's songwriting, blending introspective lyrics with rich musical textures. Meanwhile, instrumentals like

'Mudmen' showcased Wright's evocative keyboard work and Gilmour's increasingly expressive guitar playing. Listening today, it is striking how many ideas that would later flourish on 'The Dark Side of the Moon' are already present. Themes of time, mortality, memory and human experience run throughout the album.

Although rarely mentioned alongside the band's biggest releases, 'Obscured by Clouds' reached No.6 in the UK and No.46 in America, helping to establish Pink Floyd's growing international audience. For devoted fans, the album offers a unique pleasure. It captures the final moments before superstardom arrived when the band were still experimenting freely while quietly assembling the musical vocabulary that would soon transform rock history.

The Dark Side of the Moon (1973)

The Album That Changed Everything

ALBUM	RECORDED	LABEL (UK ORIGINAL)	PRODUCER(S)	RECORDING LOCATION(S)	UK PEAK	US PEAK
The Dark Side of the Moon	Jun 1972 - Jan 1973	Harvest	Pink Floyd	Abbey Road Studios, London	#2	#1

Track *Songwriter(s)*

Side One

1. **Speak to Me** *Nick Mason*
2. **Breathe (In the Air)** *Roger Waters, David Gilmour, Richard Wright*
3. **On the Run** *David Gilmour, Roger Waters*
4. **Time** *Roger Waters, David Gilmour, Richard Wright, Nick Mason*
5. **The Great Gig in the Sky** *Richard Wright, Clare Torry*

Side Two

1. **Money** *Roger Waters*
2. **Us and Them** *Roger Waters, Richard Wright*
3. **Any Colour You Like** *David Gilmour, Nick Mason, Richard Wright*
4. **Brain Damage** *Roger Waters*
5. **Eclipse** *Roger Waters*

Few albums go beyond music and become cultural landmarks. 'The Dark Side of the Moon' is one of them. Released on 1 March 1973, Pink Floyd's eighth studio album transformed the band from respected progressive rock innovators into global superstars. More than 50 years later, it remains one of the best-selling and most influential albums ever recorded.

The project grew from ideas first tested during live performances in 1972. Roger Waters conceived a thematic work exploring universal aspects of the human condition - time, greed, conflict, mortality and mental health. These themes were united by a musical sophistication that represented the culmination of everything Pink Floyd had learned over the previous decade. Recorded at Abbey Road Studios, the album benefited from cutting-edge production techniques. Engineer Alan Parsons helped create a sonic landscape unlike anything audiences had heard before. Tape loops, synthesisers, seamless transitions between songs and spoken-word interviews – such as Gerry O'Driscoll's pronouncement that,

'There is no dark side of the moon really matter of fact, it's all dark' -

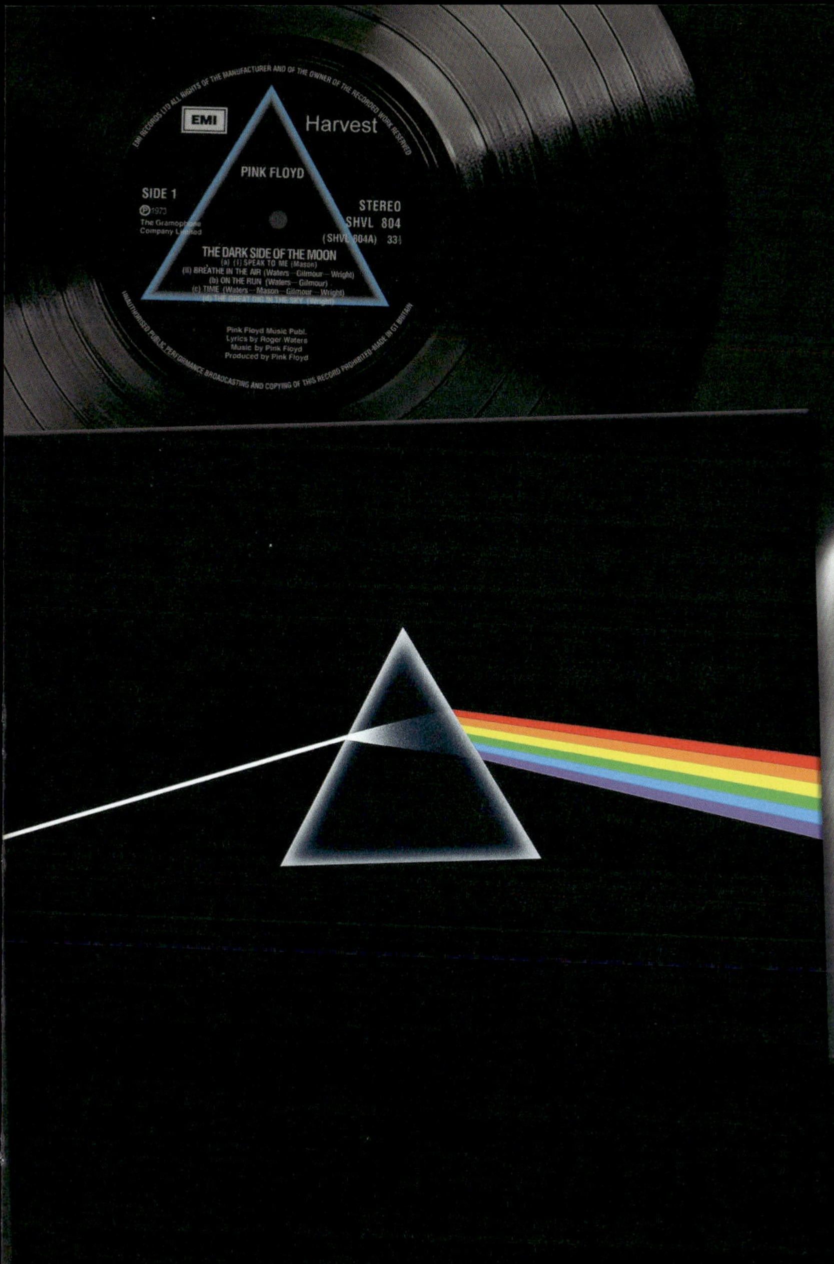

A live performance of 'The Dark Side of the Moon' at Earls Court, shortly after its release in 1973

all combined to produce a truly immersive experience.

Each track has become iconic. 'Money' transformed a cash-register rhythm into a chart hit. 'Time' confronted listeners with the terrifying speed of life passing by. 'Us and Them' blended political commentary with haunting beauty. 'Brain Damage' and 'Eclipse' brought the album to an emotionally devastating conclusion. Equally famous is the cover artwork. Designed by Hipgnosis, the prism dispersing white light into a rainbow became one of the most recognisable images in popular culture.

Commercial success was unprecedented. The album remained on the American Billboard chart for an astonishing 962 weeks and has sold more than 45 million copies worldwide. Yet statistics only tell part of the story. The real achievement lies in the album's ability to speak to successive generations. Its themes remain timeless because they address experiences shared by everyone. For many, 'The Dark Side of the Moon' is more than an album. It is an experience, a meditation on what it means to be human and one of the crowning achievements of 20th century art.

Wish You Were Here (1975)

The Ghost of Syd Barrett

ALBUM	RECORDED	LABEL (UK ORIGINAL)	PRODUCER(S)	RECORDING LOCATION(S)	UK PEAK	US PEAK
Wish You Were Here	Jan-Jul 1975	Harvest	Pink Floyd	Abbey Road Studios, London	#1	#1

Success changed everything for Pink Floyd. Following the extraordinary impact of 'The Dark Side of the Moon', the band faced a daunting question - how to follow it? The answer arrived on 12 September 1975 with 'Wish You Were Here', an album that many fans consider every bit as powerful as its predecessor. More intimate and emotional than 'Dark Side', it is a meditation on absence, loss, alienation and the corrosive effects of the music industry. At its heart, however, lies the memory of Syd Barrett. Although he had left the band seven years earlier, his presence lingered over Pink Floyd's story. The nine-part epic 'Shine On You Crazy Diamond' serves as a moving tribute to the founding member whose brilliance had illuminated the band's earliest days.

'Syd wasn't there physically, but he was there spiritually'

opined Richard Wright.

It wasn't just a spiritual presence, however. During one recording session, Barrett unexpectedly visited Abbey Road Studios in person. Almost unrecognisable due to dramatic weight gain and shaved hair, he initially went unnoticed by several members of the band. The encounter left them deeply shaken and reinforced the emotional themes running through the album. The title track remains one of the most beloved songs in rock history. Built around Gilmour's acoustic guitar and Waters' poignant lyrics, it asks deceptively simple questions about identity, authenticity and connection. Its emotional directness continues to resonate

Track *Songwriter(s)*

Side One

1. **Shine On You Crazy Diamond (Parts I-V)** *David Gilmour, Roger Waters, Richard Wright*

Side Two

1. **Welcome to the Machine** *Roger Waters*
2. **Have a Cigar** *Roger Waters*
3. **Wish You Were Here** *David Gilmour, Roger Waters*
4. **Shine On You Crazy Diamond (Parts VI-IX)** *David Gilmour, Roger Waters, Richard Wright*

decades later. Elsewhere, 'Welcome to the Machine' and 'Have a Cigar' deliver sharp critiques of the music business, portraying an industry capable of exploiting artists while reducing creativity to commerce. Roy Harper's guest vocal on 'Have a Cigar' added further character to one of the album's most memorable tracks.

Musically, the album combines grandeur with restraint. Long instrumental passages allow emotions to unfold naturally while Gilmour's guitar playing ranks among the finest of his career. Commercially, 'Wish You Were Here' debuted at No.1 on both sides of the Atlantic. Critically, its reputation has only grown with time. Many now regard it as one of Pink Floyd's most complete artistic and personal statements.

Animals (1977)

Rage, Power and the Modern World

ALBUM	RECORDED	LABEL (UK ORIGINAL)	PRODUCER(S)	RECORDING LOCATION(S)	UK PEAK	US PEAK
Animals	Apr-Dec 1976	Harvest	Pink Floyd	Britannia Row Studios, London	#2	#3

By 1977, Pink Floyd had become one of the biggest bands on the planet. Yet rather than basking in their success, they delivered one of the darkest, angriest and most uncompromising albums of their career. As David Gilmour was to say in retrospect,

'Animals was the beginning of a much more confrontational Pink Floyd.'

Track *Songwriter(s)*

Side One

1. **Pigs on the Wing (Part 1)** *Roger Waters*
2. **Dogs** *David Gilmour, Roger Waters*

Side Two

1. **Pigs (Three Different Ones)** *Roger Waters*
2. **Sheep** *Roger Waters*
3. **Pigs on the Wing (Part 2)** *Roger Waters*

Released on 21 January 1977, the album was inspired by George Orwell's 'Animal Farm' – in which dogs, pigs and sheep are used as metaphors for different groups within society. Roger Waters, increasingly becoming the band's dominant creative force, turned his attention towards themes of power, greed and social inequality. The result was a record that felt far removed from the wistful nostalgia of 'Wish You Were Here'.

The album's iconic cover featured a giant inflatable pig floating between the chimneys of London's Battersea Power Station. Designed by Hipgnosis, it became one of the most famous images in rock history. During the photo shoot, the inflatable pig famously broke free from its moorings and drifted across the skies of southern England, forcing authorities to issue aviation warnings.

Musically, 'Animals' embraced long-form composition. The three central tracks - 'Dogs', 'Pigs (Three Different Ones)' and 'Sheep' - stretch beyond 10 minutes each, allowing the band to create vast, immersive soundscapes. David Gilmour's guitar work reached new levels of intensity while Richard Wright's keyboards added layers of atmosphere and menace.

'Dogs' is widely regarded as one of the band's greatest

achievements. A bleak portrait of ruthless ambition and corporate survival, it combines soaring melodies with some of Gilmour's finest solos. 'Pigs (Three Different Ones)' takes aim at authority figures and social elites while 'Sheep' imagines the oppressed eventually rising against their masters.

The album emerged during a period of growing tension within the band. Waters was assuming greater control over songwriting while relations between the members were becoming increasingly strained. Those tensions would soon erupt during the making of 'The Wall'. Commercially, 'Animals' reached No. 2 in Britain and No. 3 in America. Although initially overshadowed by its predecessors, it has since become one of the most admired albums in the Floyd catalogue – particularly among fans drawn to its political edge and uncompromising vision. Today, 'Animals' feels remarkably contemporary. Its themes of inequality, exploitation and power remain as relevant as ever – proving that some of Waters' sharpest observations were decades ahead of their time.

The Wall (1979)

Building Rock's Greatest Monument

ALBUM	RECORDED	LABEL (UK ORIGINAL)	PRODUCER(S)	RECORDING LOCATION(S)	UK PEAK	US PEAK
The Wall	Apr-Nov 1979	Harvest	Bob Ezrin, David Gilmour, James Guthrie, Roger Waters	Britannia Row, Super Bear (France), Producers Workshop (Los Angeles), CBS Studios (New York)	#3	#1

Track *Songwriter(s)*

Side One

1. In the Flesh? *Roger Waters*
2. The Thin Ice *Roger Waters*
3. Another Brick in the Wall, Part 1 *Roger Waters*
4. The Happiest Days of Our Lives *Roger Waters*
5. Another Brick in the Wall, Part 2 *Roger Waters*
6. Mother *Roger Waters*

Side Two

1. Goodbye Blue Sky *Roger Waters*
2. Empty Spaces *Roger Waters*
3. Young Lust *David Gilmour, Roger Waters*
4. One of My Turns *Roger Waters*
5. Don't Leave Me Now *Roger Waters*
6. Another Brick in the Wall, Part 3 *Roger Waters*
7. Goodbye Cruel World *Roger Waters*

Side Three

1. Hey You *Roger Waters*
2. Is There Anybody Out There? *Roger Waters*
3. Nobody Home *Roger Waters*
4. Vera *Roger Waters*
5. Bring the Boys Back Home *Roger Waters*
6. Comfortably Numb *David Gilmour, Roger Waters*

Side Four

1. The Show Must Go On *Roger Waters*
2. In the Flesh *Roger Waters*
3. Run Like Hell *David Gilmour, Roger Waters*
4. Waiting for the Worms *Roger Waters*
5. Stop *Roger Waters*
6. The Trial *Roger Waters*
7. Outside the Wall *Roger Waters*

Few albums have captured the public imagination quite like 'The Wall'. Released on 30 November 1979, Pink Floyd's ambitious double album transformed personal trauma into one of the most spectacular and enduring works in rock history.

The story began during the exhausting 'Animals' tour. Increasingly alienated from audiences, Roger Waters found himself imagining a physical wall separating the performer from the crowd. That image became the foundation for a sprawling concept album chronicling the life of Pink, an imaginary troubled rock star who gradually withdraws from the world around him.

'The wall is what separates people from one another'

is how Waters would later explain the concept.

Drawing on his own experiences, the story explores loss, fame, war, education, isolation and psychological breakdown. The death of Waters' father during the Second World War became a particularly important theme, giving the album much of its emotional weight. Musically, 'The Wall' balances intimate moments with theatrical grandeur. Tracks such as 'Mother', 'Comfortably Numb', 'Run Like Hell' and 'Hey You' have become classics in their own right while the album's narrative structure creates an immersive listening experience unlike almost anything that had come before. The recording process was difficult. Relations between the band members had deteriorated significantly – so much so that Richard Wright left during the production. Despite these tensions, the music remained extraordinary. David Gilmour's soaring guitar solo on 'Comfortably Numb' is regularly cited among the greatest in rock history. The album's commercial success was immense. It topped charts worldwide and spawned the No.1 single 'Another Brick in the Wall (Part 2'), complete with its unforgettable children's choir. The subsequent live shows became legendary, featuring an enormous wall physically constructed across the stage before being dramatically demolished during the finale.

In 1982, the story reached cinemas through 'Pink Floyd – The Wall' starring Bob Geldof and directed by Alan Parker. The film cemented the album's place in popular culture. More than four decades later, 'The Wall' remains a cultural phenomenon. It is simultaneously a deeply personal confessional, a political statement and one of the most ambitious concept albums ever created. For many listeners, it represents the moment when Pink Floyd achieved the impossible - turning the concept of alienation into mass entertainment.

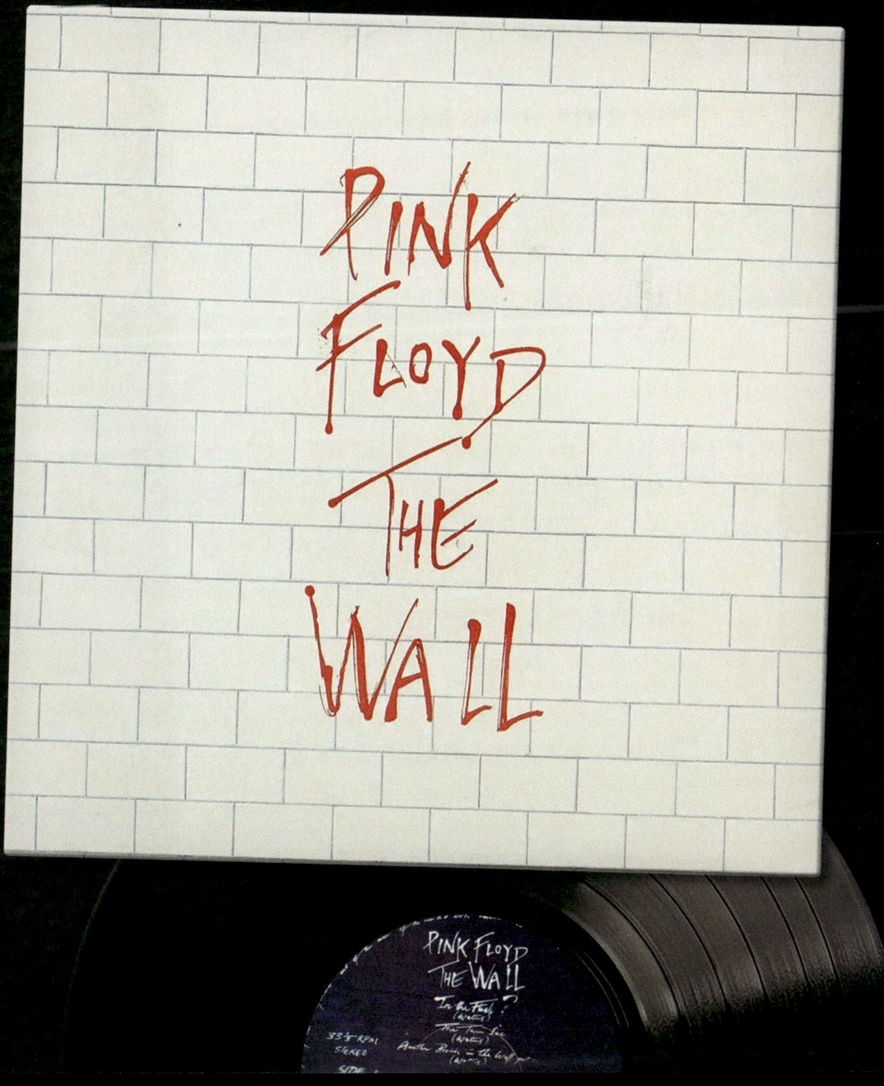

The Final Cut (1983)

A Personal Requiem

ALBUM	RECORDED	LABEL (UK ORIGINAL)	PRODUCER(S)	RECORDING LOCATION(S)	UK PEAK	US PEAK
The Final Cut	Jul-Dec 1982	Harvest	Roger Waters, James Guthrie, Michael Kamen	Mayfair Studios, Olympic Studios, Abbey Road Studios	#1	#6

Track *Songwriter(s)*

Side One

1. The Post War Dream *Roger Waters*
2. Your Possible Pasts *Roger Waters*
3. One of the Few *Roger Waters*
4. The Hero's Return *Roger Waters*
5. The Gunner's Dream *Roger Waters*
6. Paranoid Eyes *Roger Waters*
7. Get Your Filthy Hands Off My Desert *Roger Waters*
8. The Fletcher Memorial Home *Roger Waters*

Side Two

1. Southampton Dock *Roger Waters*
2. The Final Cut *Roger Waters*
3. Not Now John *David Gilmour, Roger Waters*
4. Two Suns in the Sunset *Roger Waters*

By the early 1980s, Pink Floyd were no longer functioning as a truly collaborative band. The tensions that had surfaced during 'Animals' and 'The Wall' had increased, and Roger Waters had become the group's dominant creative force. Released on 21 March 1983, 'The Final Cut' is possibly the most personal album Pink Floyd ever recorded. Subtitled 'A Requiem for the Post-War Dream', it explores themes of war, loss, political betrayal and memory. More than any previous Floyd album, it reflects Waters' own experiences and beliefs. The shadow of his father, Lieutenant Eric Fletcher Waters, who was killed in Italy during World War Two, looms large over the entire record. Waters channels decades of grief into songs that question whether the sacrifices of wartime generations achieved the peaceful and just society they had hoped to create. Tracks such as 'The Gunner's Dream', 'The Fletcher Memorial Home' and 'Two Suns in the Sunset' combine powerful storytelling with political commentary. The Falklands War and Cold War tensions provided a contemporary backdrop to Waters' reflections on conflict and leadership.

Musically, the album is more restrained than its predecessor. Rather than relying on spectacle, it

focuses on atmosphere, emotion and lyrical depth. Michael Kamen's orchestral arrangements add richness and drama while David Gilmour's guitar contributions, though limited, remain highly effective. The sessions themselves were very difficult. Relations between Waters and Gilmour were increasingly strained, and Richard Wright was no longer a full member of the band. In many respects, 'The Final Cut' feels more like a Roger Waters solo album than a Pink Floyd release. Yet despite its troubled origins, the album contains some of Waters' finest writing. Its emotional honesty and political conviction give it a unique place within the Floyd catalogue. In retrospect, 'The Final Cut' represents the end of an era. It was the final Pink Floyd album to feature Waters before his departure in 1985 and brought the band's most celebrated creative period to a close. Melancholy, thoughtful and deeply personal it remains one of the most misunderstood records in Pink Floyd's history.

A Momentary Lapse of Reason (1987)

Rebirth Against the Odds

ALBUM	RECORDED	LABEL (UK ORIGINAL)	PRODUCER(S)	RECORDING LOCATION(S)	UK PEAK	US PEAK
A Momentary Lapse of Reason	1986-1987	EMI	Bob Ezrin & David Gilmour	Astoria, Britannia Row, Mayfair, A&M Studios and others	#3	#3

Track *Songwriter(s)*

Side One

1. **Signs of Life** *David Gilmour, Bob Ezrin*
2. **Learning to Fly** *David Gilmour, Anthony Moore, Bob Ezrin, Jon Carin*
3. **The Dogs of War** *David Gilmour, Anthony Moore*
4. **One Slip** *David Gilmour, Phil Manzanera*
5. **On the Turning Away** *Roger Waters*

Side Two

1. **Yet Another Movie** *David Gilmour, Patrick Leonard*
2. **Round and Around** *David Gilmour*
3. **A New Machine (Part 1)** *David Gilmour*
4. **Terminal Frost** *David Gilmour*
5. **A New Machine (Part 2)** *David Gilmour*
6. **Sorrow** *David Gilmour*

When Roger Waters left Pink Floyd in 1985 many assumed the band was finished. Waters himself believed that Pink Floyd could not continue without him. Yet David Gilmour and Nick Mason had other ideas. Released on 7 September 1987, 'A Momentary Lapse of Reason' marked one of the most unlikely comebacks in rock history. Arriving after years of legal disputes and public disagreements, the album asked a simple question - could Pink Floyd survive without its principal lyricist? The answer was an emphatic yes.

Recorded largely aboard Gilmour's converted houseboat studio, Astoria, the album represented a fresh start. Although session musicians played a significant role and Richard Wright initially returned only as a salaried performer rather than a full member, the familiar Pink Floyd sound remained unmistakable. Sweeping keyboards, atmospheric production and Gilmour's soaring guitar work ensured continuity with the band's past while allowing a new chapter to begin. The opening track, 'Signs of Life', immediately re-established Floyd's cinematic approach before giving way to 'Learning to Fly', a triumphant anthem inspired by Gilmour's passion for aviation. The song became

one of the band's most successful late-period singles and remains a staple of classic rock. Elsewhere, tracks such as 'On the Turning Away' explored themes of compassion and social responsibility while 'Sorrow' delivered one of Gilmour's most powerful vocal performances. The latter's thunderous guitar introduction, famously recorded in a vast sports arena to capture natural echo, demonstrated the band's continuing commitment to sound experimentation.

Critics were divided. Some viewed the album as overly polished and lacking Waters' conceptual vision. Others welcomed its warmth and accessibility. Audiences were less conflicted. The record reached No.3 in both Britain and America, plus selling millions worldwide. The accompanying world tour proved even more significant. Featuring spectacular visuals, giant inflatables, lasers and state-of-the-art technology, it became one of the most successful concert tours of the decade. More importantly, it confirmed that audiences still embraced Pink Floyd regardless of internal politics. Not surprisingly Roger Waters was not impressed.

'A quite clever forgery,' was his conclusion.

Today, 'A Momentary Lapse of Reason' is increasingly appreciated as an album of renewal. Rather than dwelling on past divisions, it demonstrated resilience, proving that Pink Floyd remained a creative force capable of moving forward.

The Division Bell (1994)

The Art of Communication

ALBUM	RECORDED	LABEL (UK ORIGINAL)	PRODUCER(S)	RECORDING LOCATION(S)	UK PEAK	US PEAK
The Division Bell	1993-1994	EMI	Bob Ezrin & David Gilmour	Astoria and Britannia Row Studios	#1	#1

Track *Songwriter(s)*

Side One

1. **Cluster One** *David Gilmour, Richard Wright*
2. **What Do You Want from Me** *David Gilmour, Richard Wright, Polly Samson*
3. **Poles Apart** *David Gilmour, Polly Samson*
4. **Marooned** *David Gilmour, Richard Wright*
5. **A Great Day for Freedom** *David Gilmour, Polly Samson*
6. **Wearing the Inside Out** *Richard Wright, Anthony Moore*

Side Two

1. **Take It Back** *David Gilmour, Bob Ezrin, Nick Laird-Clowes*
2. **Coming Back to Life** *David Gilmour*
3. **Keep Talking** *David Gilmour, Richard Wright, Polly Samson*
4. **Lost for Words** *David Gilmour, Polly Samson*
5. **High Hopes** *David Gilmour, Polly Samson*

Seven years after 'A Momentary Lapse of Reason', Pink Floyd returned with an album that many regard as the strongest work of the post-Waters era. Released on 28 March 1994, 'The Division Bell' combined mature songwriting, reflective themes and some of the most elegant music of the band's later career. At its heart lay a deceptively simple idea - the difficulty of communication. Inspired partly by personal relationships and social divisions, the album explored the misunderstandings that separate individuals from one another. It was a theme that resonated deeply with the band's own history, particularly the fractures that had defined much of the previous two decades. David Gilmour worked closely with lyricist Polly Samson, who would later become his wife. Her contributions brought a fresh perspective to the songwriting, helping shape some of the album's most thoughtful and emotionally nuanced lyrics.

'The album is about people talking and not talking,' commented David Gilmour.

Opening track 'Cluster One' set the tone with an atmospheric instrumental that recalled the spacious beauty of classic Floyd. It was followed by 'What Do You Want from Me?' and 'Poles Apart' with both tracks examining relationships and human connection. The album's emotional centrepiece is undoubtedly 'High Hopes'. Closing the record on a note of wistful reflection, the song looks back on youth, memory and the passage of time. Gilmour's lap-steel guitar solo ranks among his finest performances while the lyrics evoke a powerful sense of nostalgia without descending into sentimentality. Richard Wright's presence was particularly significant. Having been absent from much of 'The Wall' and 'The Final Cut', he returned as a full member and made substantial contributions to the album's atmosphere and composition. His keyboards once again became an essential part of the Pink Floyd sound. Commercial success followed immediately. The album reached No.1 in numerous countries while the accompanying tour became one of the highest-grossing concert events of the decade. Performances from the tour would later be immortalised in the acclaimed live album 'Pulse'.

Today 'The Division Bell' is often viewed as a graceful and thoughtful late-career achievement. It may lack the cultural impact of 'Dark Side' or 'The Wall' but its emotional depth and musical craftsmanship have ensured its enduring appeal.

David Gilmour's recording studio, *Astoria*

The Endless River (2014)

A Final Farewell

For many years, 'The Division Bell' appeared destined to be Pink Floyd's final studio album. Then, two decades later came one last surprise. Released on 7 November 2014, 'The Endless River' served as both a tribute and a farewell. Built largely from previously unreleased recordings made during 'The Division Bell' sessions, the album honoured Richard Wright, who had died in 2008, while also bringing the Pink Floyd story to a poignant conclusion.

Unlike most of the band's previous releases, 'The Endless River' is predominantly instrumental. Rather than focusing on lyrics or narrative concepts, it emphasises atmosphere, texture and mood. In many ways, it recalls the exploratory spirit of albums such as 'Meddle' and 'Obscured by Clouds' thus creating a sense of coming full circle. David Gilmour and Nick Mason revisited hours of archived material, developing keyboard passages and improvisations recorded by Wright into a coherent album. The result feels less like a conventional studio release and more like a reflective journey through the band's musical DNA. The

Track *Songwriter(s)*

Side One

1. **Things Left Unsaid** *David Gilmour, Richard Wright*
2. **It's What We Do** *David Gilmour, Richard Wright, Nick Mason*
3. **Ebb and Flow** *David Gilmour, Richard Wright, Nick Mason*

Side Two

1. **Sum** *David Gilmour, Richard Wright, Nick Mason*
2. **Skins** *David Gilmour, Richard Wright, Nick Mason*
3. **Unsung** *David Gilmour, Richard Wright, Nick Mason*
4. **Anisina** *David Gilmour, Richard Wright, Nick Mason*

Side Three

1. **The Lost Art of Conversation** *David Gilmour, Richard Wright*
2. **On Noodle Street** *David Gilmour, Richard Wright*
3. **Night Light** *David Gilmour, Richard Wright*
4. **Allons-y (1)** *David Gilmour, Richard Wright*
5. **Autumn 68** *Richard Wright*
6. **Allons-y (2)** *David G*
7. **Talkin' Hawkin'** *David Gilmour, Richard Wright, Nick Mason*

Side Four

1. **Calling** *David Gilmour, Richard Wright*
2. **Eyes to Pearls** *David Gilmour, Richard Wright*
3. **Surfacing** *David Gilmour, Richard Wright*
4. **Louder Than Words** *David Gilmour, Polly Samson*

ALBUM	RECORDED	LABEL (UK ORIGINAL)	PRODUCER(S)	RECORDING LOCATION(S)	UK PEAK	US PEAK
The Endless River	1993-94 sessions, completed 2013-14	Parlophone	David Gilmour, Phil Manzanera, Martin Glover, Andy Jackson	Astoria and Medina Studios	#1	#3

opening sections flow seamlessly from one piece to another, creating an immersive listening experience. Gentle keyboard motifs, shimmering guitars and subtle percussion combine to evoke both tranquillity and melancholy. Wright's influence is everywhere. His distinctive harmonic sensibility and atmospheric playing provide the emotional heart of the album.

'Rick's voice is at the heart of this album,' David Gilmour was to later say.

The closing track 'Louder Than Words' stands apart as the record's only full vocal song. With lyrics by Polly Samson and vocals by Gilmour, it reflects on the complicated relationships that defined Pink Floyd's history. The song's central message is both simple and profound - despite disagreements, arguments and personal differences, the music endured.

Commercially, the album debuted at No.1 in numerous countries and was embraced by fans eager for one final chapter. Critics offered mixed reviews, but many recognised its value as a memorial to Wright and a graceful conclusion to an extraordinary career. More than any previous Pink Floyd album, 'The Endless River' is about memory. It looks back rather than forward - revisiting sounds, emotions and friendships that shaped one of the most influential bands in rock history. It is an entirely appropriate farewell - reflective, atmospheric, moving and unmistakably Pink Floyd.

EPILOGUE

THE LEGACY OF PINK FLOYD

Across 15 studio albums and almost five decades, Pink Floyd created one of the most remarkable catalogues in popular music. From Syd Barrett's psychedelic fantasies to Roger Waters' grand concepts and David Gilmour's soaring melodies, the band's story was one of constant reinvention. They sold more than 250 million records worldwide, produced some of the most iconic album covers ever created and transformed the possibilities of the studio album. Yet their enduring appeal lies not simply in commercial success but in their ability to tackle universal themes - time, loss, greed, conflict, memory, communication and the search for meaning.

The journey began in the underground clubs of swinging London and ended with a reflective tribute to friendship and creativity. Along the way came 'The Dark Side of the Moon', 'Wish You Were Here', 'Animals' and 'The Wall' - albums that continue to inspire new generations of listeners.

Pink Floyd's music was never merely heard, it was experienced. Vast in scale yet deeply personal, experimental yet emotionally direct, their work remains a testament to what can happen when imagination is given room to roam. As David Gilmour once observed, Pink Floyd was never really about individual personalities. It was about what happened when those personalities came together – and the result was truly extraordinary.

Pink Floyd performing on 'The Dark Side of the Moon' Tour in mid-1973